GOD'S
PLAN
for
MAN

GOD'S
PLAN
for
MAN

[Christian Doctrines in Verse]

by W. H. LITTLE

Pageant Press, Inc. *New York*

230
L72g

46030
Nov. 1963

PUBLISHED BY PAGEANT PRESS, INC.
101 FIFTH AVENUE, NEW YORK 3, NEW YORK

First Edition
Library of Congress catalog card number: 59-13333

Manufactured in the United States of America

God's Plan for Man is here set forth—
To rescue him from sin
That he might walk the way of life,
And through Christ heaven win.

Dedicated to

BIBLE STUDENTS

SUNDAY SCHOOL TEACHERS

EVERY DAY BIBLE READERS

Contents

PART I

Systematic Theology in Verse

PART II

FOREWORD

The singer of beautiful and inspiring music will always have an audience. Particularly is this so for those who "sing unto the Lord."

All of the exciting movements in the Biblical drama of Creation and Redemption have had a musical accompaniment. At the dawn of history "the morning stars (angels) sang together, and all the sons of God shouted for joy." A chorus of the heavenly denizens hailed the birth of the "Son that was given."

At history's end, it is assured by the Holy Book that there will be the "Grand Finale," when "the trumpet shall sound and the dead shall be raised incorruptible."

Listen to the world's best music—it will be glorifying and praising the life of our Lord, His deeds and His teachings. And this volume, emanating from the devout and venerable heart of Professor W. H. Little, is no exception to the profundity of soul-stirring music in poetic form.

It was my distinct honor and privilege to be a student at Lenoir Rhyne College and receive my introduction to the Arts from this Master of the Arts. Professor Little always stood before his students as the embodiment of the knowledge and truth which he taught. And they had to listen!

Professor Little possessed the happy and enviable faculty of making his subjects live challengingly and interestingly before his hearers.

It amazes me—for only a genius could do it—how Professor Little runs the gamut of biblical dogmatics from "In the beginning God" to the "Grace of our Lord Jesus Christ be with you, Amen" of Revelation.

This book, *theology in verse,* is correctly and appropriately captioned *God's Plan for Man.*

March 1, 1959

F. L. CONRAD, *D. D., President*
E. L. *Synod of North Carolina*

INTRODUCTION

RELIGIOUS POETRY

In the hymnbooks of all Christian churches poetry is recognized and used as a song for the soul. The truths conveyed in hymns and verses are imprinted upon the minds and hearts of mankind more indelibly than could possibly be expressed in the same number of words in prose form.

In many parts of the Bible, given by inspiration of God, poetry is used adding emphasis to the truths revealed. To people who appreciate poetry, of whom there are many from early childhood, prayers and songs and poetic expressions of the Christian faith often have an appeal in verse form stronger than could possibly be conveyed in prose.

Christian doctrines, poetically expressed, often give warmth to spiritual inclinations and emotions, and no doubt afford much relief from the bombardment of words current everywhere, in both secular and religious literature, in the endless flow of newspapers, magazines, and books that are rolling off the printing presses throughout our country to-day.

Poetry is coming back into its own as a private means of escaping from the tyranny of prose used so profusely in the media of communicating ideas and information. Verse in stanza forms is now being employed by businessmen, salesmen, stenographers and students to win the public ear for all kinds of commercial transactions; and this method of attracting attention is obviously effective.

Therapy is being spoken of very much nowadays for

relieving the stresses of modern life; and one of the best therapies is the medicine that brings relief and cure to distressed souls, which is found only in the proper understanding of the truths of the Christian faith as revealed to us in God's Holy Word, the Bible.

Man is an emotional creature, and poetry properly written will carry to his soul a winsome satisfaction not otherwise so readily and easily attained, particularly where the love of poetry, so spontaneous in childhood, is not wholly lost or repressed by the complexities and frustrations of our modern life.

The versification throughout this book in setting forth the Christian doctrines systematically in stanza form is that of the common meter type well known to all.

March 15, 1959   *the Author*

Part
I

Systematic Theology in Verse

PROLOGUE

The Poetic Appeal

No one as far as I do know
    Has made appeal like this—
To set in verse the Christan Faith
    For special emphasis.

Dogmatics is the term that's used
    By those who write in prose,
But that is deep and hard to read,
    As everybody knows.

From early childhood poems are read;
    They fascinate the mind;
They're found in every language known,
    And read by all mankind.

The truths that poetry conveys
    Find lodgment in the heart;
When strikingly they are made clear,
    They do not soon depart.

I trust that here in my attempt
    I shall not wholly fail,
And that the truths herein expressed
    Will those who read regale.

Truth is the bulwark of the strong;
    It elevates the weak;
It never fails to show the right
    In all we do and speak.

Whether in prose it is set forth,
    Or in impressive verse,
It is the mightiest force there is
    That's found here on our earth.

REVELATION AND THEOLOGY

Theology's a religious science;
    It deals with God and man;
It pictures a relationship
    As far as mind can scan.

Gal. 1:27, 28

It presupposes there's a God,
    Who has Himself made known,
And that mankind o'er all the earth
    Are subjects of His Throne.

Exod. 3:14

In His disclosure of Himself
    There's much man can't conceive,
For everywhere there's mystery found,
    Which he must but believe.

Eph. 3:3-5

The finite mind can't understand
    All that which God has given;
To fathom that which He's unveiled
    Man's mind has ever striven.

Eph. 3:9

God's Revelation of Himself
    Was made for man's own good,
Implanting in him a new life
    And bringing his soul food.

Col. 1:26, 27

Apart from man God is not known;
    Relationship is here;
The Holy Spirit has affirmed
    God holds all mankind dear.

I Cor. 2:4

This fact is so impressed on man
    It can't be set aside;
It is a tie so intimate
    It's felt o'er this world wide.

I Tim. 4:10

(14)

RELIGION

What is religion? Men often ask;   Rom. 8:16
 Communion 'tis, with God,
His Spirit touching man's spirit,
 Awak'ning him from nod.

Religion comes to man from heaven Heb. 2:1-3
 Revealing God's great love
Displayed to all men here on earth
 By Him who dwells above.

When Man receives this love of God, I John 4:19
 There is aroused response;
His spirit feels its warmth and glow
 And yields to it at once.

A mere hint only nature gives   Job 12:9, 10
 Of favor that's divine,
But that is really not enough
 For setting up a shrine.

There is no life communion here, Job 35:10-13
 No personality shown,
Nor anything to lift man up
 To height of God's great throne.

To make companionship a fact   I John 5:20
 There must communion be;
Obtained is this through God's dear Son,
 The Man of Galilee.

A brotherhood of saints arose,   Rev. 2
 'Twas Christ's church here on earth,
Which draws the souls of men therein
 And gives to them new birth.

THE HOLY SCRIPTURES

The Holy Bible is God's Word;　　　　　I Thess. 2:13
　　Through it He is revealed;
It opens up the Way of Life,
　　Which was before concealed.

In it God has made known to man　　　II Tim. 3:15
　　The way of truth and grace,
And how He did redeem the world
　　And brightened up its face.

Before God thus disclosed Himself　　　Rom. 1:26
　　The world in darkness lay;
There was no hope for man down here—
　　His life was one black day.

But God in pity looked on him　　　　　Eph. 5:14
　　And sent His Son to earth
Man to redeem and life restore
　　By giving him new birth.

The Saviour, Jesus Christ, was born,　　Tit. 3:4-6
　　The Christ-Child He became,
Who bore the sins of all mankind:
　　The sick, the blind, the lame.

The Bible tells of Christ, the Lord,　　John 3:16, 17
　　Man's Saviour and man's Friend,
And how He suffered for man's sin
　　That death through Him might end.

This Book was not by sages penned,　　II Pet. 1:21
　　But by the saints of old,
Who wrote as God did them inspire—
　　And not by what men told.

(16)

GOD

The foremost fact mankind conceives
    Is that a God exists;
Wherever man on earth is found,
    This idea strong persists.
	Ps. 139:7-10

No other fact's so fixed in mind,
    So present to man's thought;
It comes to him with utmost ease,
    Yes, e'en before it's sought.
	Ps. 89:6

God's being is a cosmic fact
    Sensed by men everywhere;
Among the learned and untaught,
    Though unobserved it's there.
	Ps. 113:3-8

Not needed is persuasion here;
    No evidence required;
'Tis testimony of man's heart
    Wherever thought's inspired.
	I John 5:20

It's innate in the soul of man;
    It can not be erased;
Though man has oft attempted this,
    He's failed in sad disgrace.
	I Cor. 2:11-14

No argument here can there be;
    It is a fact that's sure,
For overwhelming is the proof,
    In truth, it is secure.
	I Cor. 2:16

We are convinced there is a God,
    We ever feel Him near
And note the traces of veiled hand
    And evidences clear.
	Rom. 1:20

(17)

THE ESSENCE OF GOD

Perfections all belong to God, Who never could do wrong, Who was, and is, and is to come Immutable and strong.	Ezek. 39:7
No change in God is possible; He always is the same; He, too, is present everywhere— All honor to His Name!	Mal. 3:6
God can not sin, for He is holy; He can not lie; He's true; Nor could He e'er cease to exist— All wrongs He does eschew.	Num. 23:19
His attributes are infinite; He's present everywhere; From all eternity He reigns O'er creatures of His care.	Ps. 147:5
There is no limit to His power; There's nothing He can't do; He fills the boundless universe, And all that's therein, too.	II Chron. 2:6
As in his body man's soul lives, So lives God in His works; All creatures here He penetrates— There's nothing that He shirks!	Acts 17:24, 25
He's in the air that we here breathe, He's in the sky above; He comes to us in mercy great Through His abounding love.	Ps. 118:29

THE HOLY TRINITY

Of God the Holy Scriptures teach   II Cor. 3:14-18
   That He Himself is One,
Yet likewise clearly they reveal
   Father, Spirit, and Son.

There's a Unity and a Oneness   I John 5:7
   In the Godhead above;
Still there's disclosed plurality,
   A Trinity of Love.

The Father loved the human race;   I Pet. 1:2
   The Son did come to save;
The Holy Spirit then was given
   To draw man from the grave.

Within the Trinity of God   Eph. 2:18
   No one is more or less;
Each is a personality—
   And each we are to bless.

We pray to God our Father dear,   John 15:26
   The Son and Holy Ghost,
And yet our prayers are to one God,
   For no one is foremost.

To each belong like attributes,   Acts 17:24
   And to them we assign
Omniscience and omnipotence—
   Perfections all, divine.

The Three in Unity possess   John 14:10
   A Personality true,   16:13
And each one works in unison
   In all, that God does do.

GOD AS CREATOR OF THE UNIVERSE

The universe which we behold   Gen. 1:1
   Had once itself a birth;
There was a time when it was not—
   Long 'fore there was an earth.

The act by which it came to be   Gen. 1:2
   Is known as Creation,
When the great God omnipotent
   Gave unto it formation.

Once God existed all alone;   Ps. 90:2
   In universe was naught;
And from this nothingness was formed
   The World He shaped and wrought.

Before the act of creation   Heb. 11:3
   No thing as yet had birth,
But by His will matter appeared,
   And then was formed this earth.

The earth on which man here was placed   Ps. 146:5, 6
   Was shaped into a sphere
And all the other globes likewise,
   Which one sees far and near.

The great omnipotence of God   Ps. 19:1
   Is shown in starry skies,
Which man beholds with upward gaze
   After the sunlight dies.

These all proclaim throughout all time   Ps. 103:2-5
   The power of the Lord,
Who brought forth all things that appear
   By His creative Word.

GOD AS CREATOR OF ANGELS

The worlds that God did once create   Isa. 45:18
    Were formed for creatures all,
Who afterwards therein should dwell—
    That was before man's Fall.

God made all lives for His glory,   Ps. 19:1
    To shower on them His grace,
To share with them His attributes
    And show a loving face.

The first beings He did create   Gen. 2:1
    Were angels bright and fair,
Who lived with Him in joyful bliss
    Of love beyond compare.

The qualities bestowed on them   Ps. 103:20
    Are not in full revealed,
But they were given for His glory—
    But not to be concealed.

Servants of men they were to be;   Ps. 91:11
    In part that was the plan
As in God's Word disclosed to us,
    Which He made known to man.

The duty that they should perform   Heb. 1:14
    In this relationship
Was to serve God and mankind, too,
    In their companionship.

As finite creatures they're foremost   II Pet. 2:11
    And differ much from man,
For they're not bound to laws of space—
    They bridge voids man can't span.

(21)

GOD AS CREATOR OF MAN

By special act of Creation   Gen. 1:26
    Man's life on earth began;
Although God formed him out of dust,
    He put a soul in man.

The soul that God imparted here   Gen. 2:7
    And spirit He did give,
Divinely breathed in man's nostrils,
    Gave him the power to live.

Man's soul was perfect at the first,   Gen. 1:31
    In God's own image made;
Holy and happy was he then—
    No sin did him degrade.

A true reflection was his soul   Gen. 1:27
    Of glory God possessed;
Great were its possibilities
    If he kept God's behest.

Perfection would have been confirmed,   Ps. 8:4, 5
    Had he observed God's plan,
Which would have raised his righteousness
    To heights beyond his scan.

Sufficient strength to him was given   Gen. 2:15-17
    To overcome the force
That might obstruct his holiness
    As he pursued his course.

The plan that God designed for him   Gen. 1:27-30
    Was that he higher grow
And make ascent in righteousness
    In this life here below.

THE FALL OF ANGELS

When God called angels into life,   Neh. 9:6
   He them endowed with power;
Pure spirits were they, crowned with grace,
   Which nothing could o'erpower.

Victorious strength to them was given   Isa. 14:12-13
   To meet temptations all,
But free to them was left the choice
   To withstand test or fall.

Obeying God, they'd be unchanged,   Luke 20:36
   Would make such great advance
That they at length would reach the stage
   Where sin would find no chance.

Most angels stood the test that came;   Rev. 5:11
   A few of them did fall,
But as for heaven's multitudes
   They did not sin at all.

The first angels who disobeyed   Jude 6, 8
   Fell from their high estate,
And others, too, who followed them
   Were thrust outside the gate.

But those who did withstand the test   Ps. 103:20
   Were confirmed good and true;
Thereafter they could do no wrong,
   But only God's Will do.

Each angel stood or fell alone;   John 8:24
   Of no race was he part,
For unlike man he had no birth—
   Each sinned from choice of heart.

THE FALL OF MAN

When in the Garden, Adam lived   Gen. 1:21
   Along with his wife Eve,
Devout were they, holy, and true—
   In God they did believe.

While guidance Adam had of Him,   Gen. 2:16
   God did him freedom give,
But left him choice to act unforced
   As long as he should live.

It was God's will that man should strive   Gen. 2:17
   To make advance each day,
And to obey His Law and voice—
   And never from Him stray.

But Adam chose the other course;   Gen. 3:4-6
   From God he turned and fell;
More faith put he in Satan's claims—
   Just why, no one can tell.

In disobeying, Adam sinned,   Gen. 3:23, 24
   And veered from God away;
Hence he by Him was thrust without—
   And fell beneath sin's sway.

In Adam's Fall, all mankind fell.   Rom. 5:12
   Transmitted was his sin,
And every generation since
   To Satan is akin.

Guilt and destruction then ensued,   Rom. 5:18
   All hope for man was lost;
God's holiness was now withdrawn—
   Henceforth was man sin-tossed.

THE SIN OF ANGELS

Sin is departure from the Lord,
    From His most holy will;
'Tis straying off and doing other
    Than God's Will to fulfill.

Rom. 3:12, 13

In tracing origin of sin
    We go back of mankind
And find the first sin up in heaven—
    A sin that's undefined.

II Pet. 2:4

Before man came upon the earth,
    An angel bright and fair
Did set himself against God's will,
    And fell from heaven's care.

Jude 6

This was the origin of sin,
    The first sin that took place,
But unlike Adam's sin to come
    It did affect no race.

II Pet. 2:4
Gen. 3:1-14

Other angels also transgressed,
    One seducing another,
But they transgressed one at a time,
    Not being kin to other.

Luke 11:14, 15

What caused the first angel to fall,
    The Scriptures do not tell;
Hence one can only speculate—
    Perhaps by pride he fell.

I Tim. 3:6

Through sin his holiness was lost,
    A separation made;
Thus Satan had his origin
    When God he disobeyed.

Rev. 12:9

THE SIN OF MAN

Man's sin was disobedience,　　　　　　　Gen. 3:6
　　He failed God to obey
And fell by Satan's enticement,
　　Which thus led him astray.

He lost the purity he had　　　　　　　　Rom. 3:23
　　In mind and heart and soul,
Became the opposite of God,
　　And fell from heaven's role.

The love divine he forfeited;　　　　　　Gen. 6:5
　　His Maker he displeased;
His righteousness was not confirmed—
　　His soul was now diseased.

By disobedience he transgressed,　　　　Gen. 6:12
　　And with him the whole race;
All humankind was in first pair
　　And went down in disgrace.

Man's love of God and of His Will　　　Ps. 14:2
　　Departed from his soul,
And now he was in helplessness
　　In mastery of his goal.

He then became just otherwise　　　　　Rom. 5:12 ff
　　Than God planned he should be;
Had he withstood old Satan's snares,
　　He now would have been free.

By sinning he his freedom lost,　　　　　Deut. 31:17
　　Pursued the way of death;
His soul now severed from his God
　　Breathed thence a dying breath.

THE WAGES OF SIN

When sin took hold on soul of man,   Jas. 1:15
    And angels, too, alike,
Its penalty was by default death—
    All sinners it did strike.

All souls by Fall lapsed from God's grace,   Phil 3:18
    Could not be otherwise.
Were dispossessed of holiness
    And life beyond the skies.

Man's sin made him outcast from God;   John 3:19
    His life with Him did end;
Thenceforth his new companionship
    Was with one not his friend.

Eternal life he forfeited   Rom. 1:28 ff
    When God he disobeyed;
It could not by him be regained
    While on the earth he stayed.

Helpless was he and dead in sin,   Eph. 2:12
    He grovelled here below,   4:18, 19
Could find no happiness at all,
    Knew not which way to go.

He looked afar but found no aid;   Ps. 38:1-10
    All black to him appeared;
His sin he could not e'er uproot,
    For now his heart was seared.

A prophecy in his behalf   Gen. 3:15
    Was made before he died   Isa. 19:20
That one day would a Saviour come
    To bring man to God's side.

DEATH

As is revealed, death has two forms: Rom. 5:12
 That of the spirit first,
Then foll'wing this the physical—
 The former is the worst.

The death of spirit first took place Gen. 2:17
 The moment of the Fall,
And not when man made exit from
 This earth's revolving ball.

The turning of his soul from God Gen. 3:3
 Implanted germ of death;
'Twas this that broke companionship—
 Not breathing his last breath.

The germ imbedded in his soul Gen. 3:17 ff
 Kept growing year by year,
And finally that germ compelled
 The leaving of this sphere.

'Tis this that's known on earth as death, Rom. 5:17 ff
 Which comes to one and all;
But man's real death that came to him
 Was death of Adam's Fall.

Dead in his spirit is that man Eph. 4:18 ff
 Who does not God obey;
No longer he to Him belongs,
 With Him he can not stay.

Eternal death ensues first death Matt. 25:46
 Unless God intervene;
Nothing is there that man can do—
 No one on whom to lean.

THE OUTLOOK FOR MAN

When God brought forth angels and man,   Jas. 2:12
  He gave them strength alike
To do the right, resist the wrong—
  To do as they might like.

For all mankind since Adam's Fall   Heb. 10:1
  The outlook here was bleak;
There seemed to man no remedy
  Of which he then could speak.

Passed was the opportunity   Dan. 9:5
  Of retaining God's grace;
Man in his dire extremity
  Bore now a shameful face.

His free will hence was forfeited;   Isa. 59:2
  God's favor disappeared;
Man's choice of holiness was lost—
  By sin he was besmeared.

God's efforts for man's happiness   Rom. 7:5
  Were wrongfully repelled;
For his offense guilt must be paid,
  Which his own act compelled.

It was no fault of God Himself   Isa. 59:1, 2
  That man went to his ruin;
His free will in rejecting God
  Was but his own undoing.

God's justice could not overlook   I Tim. 2:4
  Man's falling into shame;
Yet, His great mercy had in view
  Restoring man's good name.

(29)

GOD'S PLAN OF GRACE

In Adam's Fall all mankind fell;   Ps. 14:2, 3
    His holiness was lost;
Utter destruction he now faced—
    Freedom his fall did cost.

To be confirmed there was no chance;   Eph. 2:11, 12
    His free will now was gone;
Before him stood his guilt and shame—
    The seed of sin was sown.

Without a miracle from heaven,   Rom. 7:18-24
    Before him lay no hope,
Nor could there be recovery
    In human power or scope.

God had done all that He could do   Rom. 1:18-25
    For man's own future good
To raise him to a higher plane
    Where he'd eat angels' food.

But man looked down upon the earth,   Rom. 1:28-32
    Upon the things of time,
And did not gaze out in the blue
    To seek a happier clime.

It was his sin that caused his fall,   2 Pet. 3:9
    Not any fault of God;
Yet God in pity infinite
    Besought man 'neath sin's rod.

God's justice called for punishment;   John 3:14-17
    Mercy constrained His heart;
Redemption now must be devised,
    Or both will stay apart.

(30)

GOD'S ETERNAL PURPOSE

A plan of grace for fallen man   Acts 2:29-36
     Was in the heart of God,
Who foreknew consequence of sin
     Would put him 'neath the sod.

'Twas God's will from eternity   I Pet. 1:2-20
     To rescue man from sin,
And with that plan devised in love
     He sought to redeem him.

Redemption is no afterthought,   Rom. 8:28, 29
     Revealing God's great love,
For that was long predetermined
     In His foresight above.

To show God's love was this world made,   Isa. 43:7
     For its divine display,
And not a prison cell for man
     Forever and for aye.

'Twas made for man's earthly abode,   Ps. 19:1
     A halo of God's glory,
And not a place for punishment—
     Nor for a tragic story.

That which was lost in Adam's Fall   Rom. 5:20
     In Christ was more than gained,
For where in man sin did abound,
     Grace greater was attained.

In rank of God's creative work   Heb. 2:7
     Man was angels beneath,
But in His plan of redemption
     He'll him a crown bequeath.

THE PLAN OF SALVATION

Redemption through God's plan for Man   John 3:16
    Is offered now to all,
Embracing every human life
    Since day of Adam's Fall.

By nature man's a child of wrath,   Rom. 3:24
    By grace a child redeemed;
Where no resistance here takes place,
    God's grace on him is beamed.

God from eternity has known   II Thess. 2:13
    Those who'll His grace receive,
Which in the Christ is given to all
    If only they'll believe.

Jesus was born mankind to save   I Thess. 5:9, 10
    From sin, anguish, and death;
He paid the debt man could not pay
    E'en to his dying breath.

The plan devised was one of love,   Gal. 1:4
    God's Son became a man,
Who by His death atonement made
    For all beneath sin's ban.

The punishment imposed for guilt   Rom. 10:4-10
    Was borne by Him for all;
And every one who this believes
    Accepts His gracious call.

No soul is saved but by His blood   I Pet. 1:18, 19
    So freely shed for man;   I Tim. 2:4
And if a soul is ever lost,
    It must refuse God's plan.

PROVIDENCE

O'er all extends God's Providence; Jer. 10:12, 13
 It's seen on every hand,
Embraces the whole universe:
 The sun, the stars, and land.

The center of this Providence Mat. 6:26-33
 Relates alone to man,
Concerns redemption from his sins,
 Removes from him its ban.

God's creation of man on earth Gen. 8:22
 Reveals intent in view;
Likewise, His preservation gives
 Safe life to me and you.

Against disrupting influence Ps. 107:2-14
 God does here interpose
And from destruction saves mankind,
 And from all mortal woes.

The workings of His Providence I Pet. 3:12
 To souls of men pertain,
For it is ever God's design
 That man His grace attain.

In all things right God does concur; Acts 17:28
 He acts in all that act;
His Spirit breathes in every breeze,
 And blooms in flowers, in fact.

Without God's power man can do naught, II Cor. 9:8
 For He is Lord of all;
There's no salvation without Him
 From Adam's sin and Fall.

(33)

REDEMPTION

"When fulness of the time was come,"   Gal. 4:4, 5
    God sent His Son to earth
Man to redeem and life restore
    By giving him "New Birth."

This was the myst'ry long concealed   I Pet. 1:18-21
    In boundless mind of God,
Which was at length revealed in Christ,
    Who saved man from sin's rod.

The Incarnation of the Christ   Col. 1:14
    In point of time took place
When He was born in Bethlehem,
    A Son of David's race.

A Saviour He became for man,   Heb. 9:15
    Invited all to come,
Partake the riches of His grace
    And find a heavenly home.

When He was asked about Himself,   John 5:39
    This was His prompt reply:
"Go search the Scriptures for my claim"—
    "Of Me they testify!"

God's only Son became the Christ,   Matt. 20:28
    Who will His people save
And bring them back to His abode,
    Where sin can not deprave.

The mystery of all myst'ries   Eph. 1:7-14
    Above and beyond thought
Is that of man redeemed by Christ
    Through His atonement wrought.

(34)

Before the Christ came down to earth   Matt. 1:20, 21
 An angel did reveal
That He, the Son of God, would come
 And man's deliv'rance seal.

This was God's plan devised in love   Tit. 2:14
 To rescue man from sin;
Christ would redeem him back to God—
 His soul from Satan win.

"Jesus" He was by kindred called   Matt. 1:20-23
 The name by angel given,
Who'd come to earth to save all men—
 And bring them up to Heaven.

The Son of God became the Christ,   II Tim. 1: 9, 10
 When Jesus here was born;
The Divine and the human type
 Have raised salvation's horn.

In Christ there is but one "ego,"   John 10:32-38
 That "Ego's" God, the Word,   John 1:1
Who with the Father and Holy Ghost,
 Is God whom Adam heard.

Jesus was God and yet was Man,   I Tim. 2:5
 Two natures joined in One;
'Tis far beyond our human thought—
 A new life's here begun!

We can not understand the mode;   I Pet. 1:16
 We must accept the fact,
For we can't go beyond God's Word—
 Nor can from it subtract!

THE PERSON OF THE CHRIST

The personal'ty of the Christ	Rom. 9:5
When here He had His birth	
Was diff'rent from the humankind,	
That e'er was born on earth.	

For when man's Saviour here appeared	John 1:14
Incarnation occurred;	Rom. 1:3, 4
The person, though, in Jesus Christ	
Was the eternal Word.	

In Him two persons there were not,	Rom. 8, 3
The Person was Divine;	
The human nature Christ assumed	
Made man of diff'rent kind.	

His earthly nature was true man	Gal. 4:4, 5
Endowed by the Divine	
With all the powers and attributes	
The natures could combine.	

Confused were not body and soul	Eph. 3:9
In this mysterious union,	
For indivisible are they now—	
There's here intercommunion.	

The life Divine in Jesus Christ	John 20:31
Is that which gives Him worth,	
Enabled Him to bear man's sin	
When He was here on earth.	

Jesus, the Christ, has power unmatched;	Matt. 11:28-31
Save can He all mankind;	
His invitation ever is:	
"Come all, both sick and blind."	

(36)

THE HUMAN NATURE OF CHRIST

The human nature Christ possessed   John 1:14
   Once did begin to be;
'Twas formed in womb of virtuous maid,
   Who lived in Galilee.

Selected was a virgin pure   Isa. 7:14
   For this honor divine,
Descendant of the patriarchs—
   Heir of King David's line.

'Fore Mary was espoused to man   Luke 1:28-30
   An angel to her came,
Revealed to her that she should be
   A woman of great fame.

By Highest Power she should become   Luke 1:31-35
   The blessed Saviour's mother,
For unto her should babe be born
   Who would be mankind's brother.

The Christ of God the Babe would be,   Luke 1:76-79
   Whom prophets did foretell
Would come to save this wicked world
   From endless pains of hell.

In Bethlehem of old Judea   Matt. 2:6
   In days of Herod, King,
The wondrous event of this birth
   Did through that region ring!

Jesus, the Christ, was born a Babe,   Matt. 1:21, 25
   The Ruler of mankind;
To man He would Redeemer be,
   Restore his soul and mind.

THE STATE OF HUMILIATION

When God's Son was in human flesh,   Matt. 28:18
    He reigned just as before;
The Father, Son, and Holy Ghost
    Ruled as in days of yore.

E'en while a Babe in Bethlehem   I Tim. 6:14, 15
    Almighty power was His,
For He with them upheld the world
    And all that therein is.

Until redemption was complete,   John 18:36, 37
    He bore humility;
His human nature made no show—
    Yet had ability.

Possessing attributes of God,   Phil. 2:5-9
    It could have made display,
But abstained from full use of them
    Throughout His earth-time stay.

The state of humiliation   Mark 13:32
    It's called in church's lore;
His human nature did not use
    The power it held in store.

In Christ the "Ego" could not change,   Heb. 13:8
    Become greater or less,
That change was in His human flesh—
    All power it did possess!

While Christ humiliation bore,   I Pet. 2:21-24
    His human nature drooped;
To restrain itself it was forced—
    For dying it had stooped!

(38)

THE STATE OF EXALTATION

With Christ's resurrected body
    Begins His exaltation;
Henceforth His body is now free
    In its divine relation.

                Rom. 1:3, 4

In His reanimated flesh
    He from the grave arose,
But in a glory greater far
    Than e'er He did disclose.

                I Pet. 3:18, 22

He suffers hence from man no more,
    But rises in His strength;
He yields not now to any foes,
    But keeps them at arms' length.

                Acts 2:33

No more can they lay hold on Him,
    His body hence is free
To come or e'en to disappear
    At will, where'er He be.

                Rom. 6:9

From thence it holds itself not back,
    His body's glorified,
A power it exercises now,
    Which was before denied.

                Luke 24:36-51

The attributes it now displays
    In union with Divine,
Gave to His form a radiant glow—
    From thence His face did shine.

                John 1:14

At His Ascension this beamed forth
    In fascinating light,
When Jesus Christ, man's Saviour, rose
    Into the heav'nly height.

                Acts 1:9, 10

(39)

OFFICE OF CHRIST AS PROPHET

The Saviour human, yet divine,   Acts 7:55, 56
   Who came to earth to die,   Heb. 2:9
Arose from grave with radiant glow,
   Then made ascent on high!

Three missions here His life fulfills: John 1:29-34
   As Prophet He proclaims,
As Priest He is our Advocate,
   As King o'er us He reigns.

From heaven He was the Teacher sent   John 20:31
   To make known unto man
The way of life, salvation free,
   Which through Him God did plan.

Out from the cloud came God's command: Matt. 17:5
   "Hear Him!" that voice did cry;
Redemption it proclaimed for man
   That he no more should die!

As Prophet teaching things divine,   John 1:18
   He preached the Word of Life,
Which draws mankind from sin and shame
   And puts an end to strife.

Without a fault His teachings are!   John 6:69
   Mistake He can not make,
For wisdom from above He brings,
   Of which all should partake.

True meaning gave He to the Law,   John 19:36, 37
   Freed it from hoary past,
Expounded the two Testaments
   And proved their truths would last.

(40)

Christ's special work as Prophet was   John 6:68, 69
　　The Gospel to proclaim
To set forth free forgiveness to
　　All who'll accept His Name.

The plan God wrought for saving man   Matt. 11:28
　　Bids sinners to Him come
And place their burdens on the Christ,
　　Founder of Christendom.

His work as Prophet's not confined   Mark 16:15, 20
　　To words from His own mouth,
For He ordained that they be preached
　　In north, east, west, and south.

"Who heareth you, he heareth Me,"   Luke 10:16
　　He here gives us His seal;
If this is done as He commands;
　　'Twill bring great joy and weal.

He by His Spirit gives us power   Acts 1:8
　　To sound His praises high,
And bids all men come unto Him
　　That they might never die.

His promise is, He'll not refuse   Luke 15:20-24
　　The man who seeks His face;
He'll be more ready to hear him
　　Than man to seek His grace.

Where'er this Gospel is proclaimed,   I Cor. 1:18-23
　　Through it the power He'll give
To accept Christ's atonement wrought
　　That man through Him might live.

OFFICE OF CHRIST AS PRIEST

As Prophet Christ was unequalled,
    But as Priest stands as high,
For He from Heaven came down to earth
    For sinful man to die.

              Eph. 1:7

Of all the priests that ever lived
    He is the one High Priest;
But when you see His lowly life,
    You'd think He was the least.

              Heb. 10:11-13

From God's exalted throne He came
    To be a Priest for man,
To give His life upon a tree—
    A myst'ry none can scan.

              Heb. 10:19-22

Man here on earth, created pure,
    Had fallen into sin,
Had disobeyed His Maker, God—
    Was now wretched within.

              Eph. 4:18

In this condition he was lost;
    There was no help in sight;
He could not now to God return—
    Most dismal was his plight.

              2 Thess. 1:9

In mercy God looked down on man,
    The creature of His hand,
Who in his fallen state was lost—
    He had no home or land.

              Ezek. 33:11

Then God sent down His only Son
    To rescue him and save,
To pave the way and bring him back—
    Now sin cannot enslave!

              Eph. 2:15, 16

As Priest Christ made amends to God,
   Offered Himself as Lamb
For all the sins of mankind here—
   Who can it understand?

He came down here to take man's place,
   To save man's soul from sin,
To open up a paradise
   That he might enter in.

Christ died upon an earthly tree,
   Burdened with guilt of man,
And in His body paid sin's debt,
   And lifted heaven's ban.

He made atonement for man's sin
   By suff'ring in his stead,
That He might life to him restore—
   For all mankind He bled!

He was both Priest and Sacrifice,
   The Giver and the Gift,
Who gave Himself vicariously
   To heal for man sin's rift.

The sacrifice that He endured
   Met all the Law's demands;
He did this voluntarily
   To fill for man God's plans.

For sin He paid the penalty
   Which man was due to pay,
And rescued him from punishment
   Where hope shed not a ray.

John 1:29

John 14:2

Matt. 26:28

Luke 19:10

Heb. ? 14-18

Heb. 2:17

Rom. 5:8

What Christ endured on Cross for man　　　Acts 2:23, 24
　　Was death, cruel, intense;
The anguish deep that He there bore
　　Was sin's tortures immense.

While He was hanging on the Tree　　　Isa. 53:4-11
　　The weight of this world's sin
Crushed down upon His righteous soul
　　And cramped His heart within.

Sustained was He by God's own power　　　Col. 1:20 ff
　　To bear the crushing load,
Else we would ever have been lost
　　And hence missed heaven's road.

Thus full atonement has been made　　　Heb. 2:17
　　For man's eternal death
When Christ, our Priest, suffered for us
　　'Twixt birth and dying breath.

Redemption this the Scriptures call,　　　Eph. 1:7
　　The price Christ paid for sin;
The myst'ries here are so profound
　　We can not enter in!

The blessings of eternal life　　　Rev. 5:9
　　Are now ours to enjoy;
Our souls are peaceful and at rest—
　　Sin can no more destroy.

The great God who created us　　　Col. 1:14 ff
　　Sinless, holy, and pure,
Has brought us back into the fold—
　　From guilt we're now secure!

(44)

When we accept the Saviour Christ;   I Pet. 1:18, 19
 With Him we exchange place;
He died for us, the guilty ones—
 We through His death have grace.

Wounded was He for our offense;   Isa. 53:5
 He for our sins was bruised;
On Him was laid our chastisement—
 In Him we're not refused.

Herein is love—not that we loved,   I John 4:10
 It's mercy pure expressed;
Infinite were His sufferings,
 Yet made He no protest!

He gave His life to bring man back   John 3:16
 To His great Father's Home,
And thus redeemed man need not now
 Be lost or ever roam.

All has been done that God could do;   John 3:18
 It is now up to man;
If only he'll but Christ accept,
 Freed he'll be from sin's ban.

Our great High Priest is now in Heaven,   II Tim. 4:18
 Us He invites to come,
And if to Him our hearts we yield,
 He'll bring us to His Home.

He's praying at His Father's Throne,   Rom. 8:34
 For us He intercedes
That we be kept from snares of sin—
 This for us He now pleads.

OFFICE OF CHRIST AS KING

King was Christ at Incarnation,
    Was born King of the Jews,
Was by the Magi honored King,
    Which Pilate did refuse.

John 18:36, 37

On first Palm Sunday multitudes
    Did His name greatly praise,
Shouting to Him their loud hosannahs
    In anthems of sweet lays.

John 12:13

With joyful voice they hailed Him King,
    Extolled His mighty acts;
To Honor Him they did not fail—
    His miracles were facts.

John 12:13
Ps. 72:17-19

Before Pilate He did assert
    His Kingship o'er the world,
And Pilate sought Him to release,
    But weakness he unfurled.

Matt. 27:11-23

The superscription on the Cross
    Proclaimed Him as a King;
'Twas written in three languages—
    His foes this truth did sting.

Luke 23:38

Raised far above all power and might,
    All things beneath His feet,
Christ's mediatorial work ends not
    Before it is complete.

Eph. 1:19-23

His Kingdom grows from age to age,
    We pray "Thy Kingdom come";
A great rejoicing there will be
    When Christ His own brings home.

Rev. 5:11-13

(46)

THE KINGDOM OF GOD

Christ sits at the right hand of God; I Cor. 15:24 ff
    A member of our race
Is now enthroned high up in heaven,
    And rules with power and grace.

Complete is our redemption now, 2 Cor. 5:18 ff.
    But it's to be applied;
By man it must be heralded
    O'er this world far and wide.

Christ's Kingdom is not simply power, Luke 8:1
    Mere majesty and grace;
It's organized to bring man back
    To a sweet resting place.

No other kingdom's thus arranged Dan. 7:14
    Like His Kingdom above,
Which seeks to draw the souls of men
    To His abode of Love.

His world-wide Kingdom reaches out; Luke 1:68-75
    It becks to one and all
To shake off sin and Satan's snares
    And heed the Saviour's call.

The Gospel of salvation free I John 5:13-15
    Proclaims that "God is Love,"
And that He will no man debar
    From His Kingdom above.

There's nothing that can withstand God; Rom. 8:37-39
    He conquers hearts and lives,
And bursts the bonds of sin's tight grip,
    When His Word there arrives.

(47)

THE HOLY SPIRIT

The Holy Spirit has been given   John 3:5
   To bring redemption home
To minds and hearts of all mankind,
   Wherever they may roam.

Before the Day of Pentecost   John 7:39
   His presence was not felt
Except, quite rare, at certain times,
   When with His saints He dwelt.

On Pentecostal Day He came   John 14:16
   Aft Christ was glorified;
In fullest measure He appeared
   When He came to abide.

In special form and brilliancy   Acts 2:3
   He loomed as flame of fire,
Which sat on head of each one there—
   Great zeal it did inspire!

Such inspiration ne'er was stirred   Acts 2:4
   As they felt there that day;
The wonders of redeeming love
   They preached without delay.

Jesus, the Christ, was crucified   Acts 2:22-28
   Just fifty days before;
It then looked like all had been lost —
   But now the gain was more.

The Comforter whom Christ foretold   Acts 2:31-33
   Before He went away
Into the heavens above the sky,
   Was now come down to stay.

(48)

The new life here that then burst forth   Rev. 21:3, 4
    Was like a warm spring day
Foll'wing a winter with its cold,
    Which took man's cheer away.

On day that Christ took leave of earth   Acts 1:4
    And bade "His own" good-bye;
In solemn words He promised them
    He'd send power from on high.

His presence with them vanished then;   Luke 24:51
    In glory He had gone;
They felt the need of one to lead—
    Were helpless all alone!

They had no record of His work,   Luke 24:13-15, 45
    Nor of the words He said;
Their mem'ries now were blackened out—
    Their hearts were filled with dread!

At Pentecost a power came down,   Acts 2:3, 4
    It was the Holy Ghost,
Who transformed them in heart and will
    Into a mighty host!

Their darkened mem'ries now began   Acts 4:31
    To take on rays of light;
They called to mind all Christ had said
    And preached the Word with might!

Jesus who died and rose again   Acts 4:33
    Proclaimed they unafraid
As Christ, the Saviour of mankind,
    Whom wicked hands had slayed.

His Resurrection they affirmed:
    That He arose from grave
And now sits at right hand of God,
    Who seeks all men to save.

Acts 2:24

The Apostles all and foll'wers, too,
    Did spread the "Gospel News"
That Christ had come man to redeem
    And wills not one to lose.

Acts 5:42

The "Glad Tidings" that they proclaimed
    While here they trod the earth
Was laden with the Spirit's power,
    Which brought to them "new" birth.

I Cor. 2:9

The influence of the Word they preached
    Had warmth before unknown;
It burned its way in human breasts—
    E'en to marrow and bone.

Heb. 4:12

Before God's Word was thus enriched,
    It carried only hope,
But now realities were seen,
    Which widened out man's scope.

I Cor. 2:9, 10

God's Word attests to all mankind
    Who hear the Gospel call,
That Christ is Lord o'er all the world,
    And wills to save them all.

Acts 26:16-20

Since Christ is set at God's right hand
    And now withdrawn from men,
He writes His Law within their hearts—
    But not with ink and pen.

Heb. 8:10

The general message of God's grace   II Tim. 3:15
    Is individualized;
Man's soul is freed from mortal sin,
    His guilt's not penalized.

Christ's message has convincing power   Heb. 4:12
    Whenever it is heard
Because God's Spirit dwells therein,
    It truly is God's Word.

By it Christ's Kingdom here is spread   Ps. 43:3
    Wherever it is preached;
And it's the Lord's intense desire
    That all mankind be reached.

His Spirit moves men to proclaim   Mark 16:20
    The Holy Word divine,
Which conquers sin and gives new life—
    Brings sight to inly blind.

On this pure Word, Christ's church is based;   Eph. 2:18-22
    By it she is built up,
And through her ministrations wrought,
    Men will with their Lord sup.

Throughout eternity they'll dine;   I Cor. 2:4-9
    New views will e'er unfold,
And showers of blessings there will be—
    Richer than streams of gold.

There they fore'er with Christ shall be,   Thess. 4:17
    Their Saviour and their King,
Where all is joy and blessedness—
    Where sweet hosannahs ring!

THE WORD

The sole Revealer of all time   Heb. 1:2
     Is Jesus Christ, the Lord,
Who heaven's myst'ries has unveiled
     Through His inspiring Word.

The Saviour Christ gave to the world   Acts 13:39
     That new best Word of Life,
Which tells of man's redemption here
     That saves him from sin's strife.

God's revelation was complete   Heb. 1:3
     When Christ was taken up
From foot of old Mount Olivet,
     Aft He had drained the cup.

His suff'ring now for sin was o'er;   Heb. 2:14
     Redemption's work was done,
Accomplished was His purpose here—
     His earthly life was spun.

The Word He preached while here on earth   Luke 1:1-4
     Was to Apostles taught;
But aft He left they were inspired
     To write down every thought.

God's Spirit guided those who wrote,   II Tim. 3:16
     Preserving the whole truth
That no corruption entered in,
     Nor additions, forsooth.

Directed of the Lord were they   Matt. 28:19-21
     In all they did and said;
With power to preach were they sent forth
     O'er all the world to tread.

(52)

The truths taught them by Jesus Christ   Acts 16:10
    Would ever present be;
In minds and hearts they would remain—
    The truth would set them free.

'Twas not their message they proclaimed,   II Cor. 4:5
    But God's Word to them given
By Jesus Christ while with them here,
    Who now from them was riven.

"Who heareth you, he heareth me,"   Luke 10:16
    Said He to them one day;
Assurance strong it gave to them—
    It cast a heav'nly ray.

First with their voice they preached the Word   Acts 18:26-28
    As long as they had strength,
And afterwards, as age advanced,
    They wrote it down at length.

Clear inspiration they possessed   John 15:26, 27
    Beneath the Spirit's sway,
Which from all error them preserved—
    They could not go astray.

The Word they penned was not their word,   II Pet. 1:21
    But God's from up on high;
They viewed it not as their own thoughts—
    This they all testify.

As long as Christ's Apostles lived,   II Tim. 3:15-17
    The Word, too, lived, likewise,
But God ordained it written down
    For generations' rise.

For mankind all the Word was meant   Ps. 19:2-4
    And not for one lifeline,
But for all peoples, tongues, and tribes
    On which the sun does shine.

As voucher of its purity,   I Cor. 4:15-17
    To keep it as God's own,
Unaltered as Apostles spoke,
    It must to man be shown.

On oral word one can't depend;   Tit. 1:9-11
    It must be copied down;
Transmitted thus from age to age,
    It's held in great renown.

Through spoken Word or written Word,   John 6:63
    Which we from Christ receive,
The Holy Spirit ever works
    And stirs man to believe.

Man's heart the Word regenerates   Rom. 8:1-14
    And makes him clean within;
Away from earth it draws his soul
    And frees him from his sin.

Where'er God's Word is thus proclaimed,   Acts 10:42-44
    In sermon, prayer, or song,
The Spirit there pours out His grace,
    And helps weak men grow strong.

For all mankind the Word's been given   John 17:14-17
    To bring them back to life,
To draw them up to heaven above
    From this world's sin and strife.

LAW AND GOSPEL

The Law and Gospel are God's Word,   II Tim. 2:15
   And each has its own sphere;
'Tis God's command that both be preached
   If man His Word would hear.

The Law sets forth the will of God,   Luke 10:25-28
   It tells what man should be
And what he should or should not do,
   If he'd keep himself free.

The Gospel is "Good News" God sends   John 20:31
   To men in Satan's chains,
Whose souls are dead to holiness
   And can but suffer pains.

It brings to them a righteousness,   Rom. 4:21-25
   Not one of their own kind,
But that of their Redeemer, Christ,
   Who died for all mankind.

The Law commands that man love God   Matt. 22:37
   With mind and heart and soul;
If that's not in his power to do,
   He'll miss the heavenly goal.

It, too, commands that love to others   Matt. 22:39
   Shall equal that of self,
That one should not fail to give aid,
   Nor covet other's pelf.

For least defect in keeping them   Jas. 2:10
   The penalty is death;
The Law permits no infraction
   E'en to one's dying breath.

Man in his natural state of sin   Rom. 7:14-21
    Since day that Adam fell,
Cannot perform the Law's commands—
    He's in a prison cell.

But heaven's "Good News" the Gospel brings,   Rom. 8:1-5
    Shows him a clear way out;
The Saviour, Christ, from up above
    Will for him Satan rout.

The Saviour came, the Holy One,   Tit. 2:14
    The Son of God on high,
To take man's place and him redeem
    And fit him for the sky.

For man Christ was a substitute   Gal. 3:13
    To keep the Laws' demands;
These He observed in every jot
    In all of its commands.

He won for man a righteousness   Eph. 2:18-22
    To transfer o'er to him,
Which would enable him to stand
    Before God freed from sin.

This mantle of pure righteousness,   Rev. 19:8
    Won solely for mankind,
Becomes the garment man puts on,
    Which hides his sin behind.

When man accepts this righteousnes   Phil. 3:9
    So freely offered him,
He can save face before his God
    In light that is not dim.

By bitter suff'rings and His death   Isa. 1:18
   Christ paid for sin's deathblow,
And "though our sins be crimson red
   They shall be white as snow."

If man believes, he need not fear,   Rev. 3:10
   Nor ever dread despair,
For Christ is ready, if besought,
   To take him in His care.

All terrors of the Law are o'er;   Gal. 3:11, 12
   Redemption is complete;
The favor now of God is his—
   He will not sin repeat.

In Christ now rests man's confidence;   Job 19:25
   The grace of God is felt;
He'll not be punished for his sins—
   A lash will not be dealt.

For Christ's sake God forgives them all,   Tit. 2:11-14
   Restores man's peace and joy;
Sadness and sorrows are dispelled—
   Sin can no more destroy.

Henceforth he'll ever strive to be   Tit. 2:10
   Disciple of his Lord,
And keep the faith throughout his life
   In meekness and accord.

And then when struggling days are o'er,   Matt. 25:34
   He'll hear the glad acclaim
"Come up, thou faithful one in Christ,"
   Give praise to His great Name.

WORD AND SACRAMENTS

The Word of God comes to mankind	Acts 2:41
In two especial ways:	
Testimony of Apostles	
And sacramental phrase.	

Through God's Word and its Sacraments   Acts 8:12, 13
   The Holy Spirit works;
He uses them as instruments—
   In them His Spirit lurks.

The preaching of His Holy Word   Matt. 28:19, 20
   Was by Himself ordained;
To bring to man Christ's Atonement,
   This Word's to be proclaimed.

Two ways there are in which 'tis done;   Acts 10:44-48
   There's diff'rence 'twixt the two:
The one is audible and preached,
   The other plain to view.

The visible is what we see   Acts 2:38
   In the Sacraments we know;
Through Baptism and the Eucharist
   God does His grace bestow.

The Word outside and Word inside   Mark 16:16
   Are in two modes applied;
They both are means of channeling
   Redemption's "gladsome tide."

The general and the specific   Matt. 28:19
   Express the ways we know,
But there is here a difference—
   God's own Word tells us so.

As is revealed in Holy Writ,   Luke 4:43, 44
    And, too, when it men preach,
The voice of God is general,
    Like that in public speech.

God's mercy is to us declared   John 3:16, 17
    To one and all alike;
There are no men excluded here
    Save those that 'gainst Him strike.

From all-embracing promises   Mark 16:15, 16
    One must himself infer
That what is offered to all men
    Could to him, too, refer.

An inference from a world-wide pledge   II Tim. 1:12
    Oft fails to inspire glee;
It is more reassuring far
    To know that it means "me"!

To give assurance beyond a doubt   Heb. 10:16-22
    Sacraments were devised,
And when by personal touch received,
    One knows he is comprised.

Baptism with water and the Word   I Pet. 3:21
    Gives confidence complete
That God is seeking to bring *me*
    Unto His mercy-seat.

In cov'nant with my God in Christ   Matt. 23:37, 38
    Still, I may not be saved,
For if I thrust the Christ aside,
    I choose to stay depraved.

In Body and the Blood of Christ,   Mark 14:22-25
   Of which I oft partake,
I find assurance doubly sure
   He'll not my soul forsake.

Instead "Christ died for all mankind,"   Eph. 2:13-20
   I know "Christ died for me";
I can not doubt it any more—
   The proof's Gethsemane!

I've taken Him into my mouth;   I Cor. 10:16, 17
   His body's touched my tongue;
Complete is now my confidence —
   May His praise e'er be sung!

In Sacrament I him partake,   I Cor. 11:23-26
   The Son of God on high,
And in receiving I'm assured
   I shall not ever die.

All doubt's dispelled, I'm now convinced   John 20:27-29
   That Christ will me receive
Into His Kingdom up above,
   For in Him I believe.

He paid the guilt of all my sins;   Phil. 3:9-14
   A righteousness He's won;
Which is to me, His child, transferred
   Until my journey's run.

Thus by God's grace His love is sealed   Rom. 8:31-39
   In His great gift to me;
The heavenly home I know I'll reach
   When here I cease to be.

BAPTISM

Baptism is termed a Sacrament,
 The first one of the two
That Jesus for mankind ordained,
 Man's old life to make new.

Rom. 6:4-18

The earthly form is water pure,
 Connected with God's Word,
Applied according to command
 Where Christ's mandate is heard.

John 3:5

It individualizes man,
 Proves God desires his soul,
Proclaims that He is seeking him,
 And wants to make him whole.

Acts 2:38 ff

The one baptised, adult or child,
 Is given this firm pledge
That he to God alone belongs—
 This Scripture does allege.

Gal. 3:27

Each drop of water used therein
 Assures him of God's love,
And that he's brought in covenant
 With the great God above.

Gal. 3:26-29

He can not his salvation doubt
 When water is applied
In name of Jesus Christ, his Lord,
 Who for him on Cross died.

Mark 16:16

In his baptism he holds the proof
 That heaven's blessings all
Have been provided for his soul—
 No curse can him befall!

Rom. 6:3-11

The efficacy of his Baptism   Acts 2:38, 39
    Rests solely on God's Word
With which it is connected here—
    No human power concurred.

Through it the Spirit sanctifies   John 17:17
    By making use of truth,
Which taught by elders is soon learned
    By every baptised youth.

The remembrance of his baptism   Acts 20:31, 32
    To him's a stream of grace
Because the Word therein applied
    He does by faith embrace.

'Tis not remembrance of the water   Tit. 3:5-7
    That did there touch his brow,
Nor hand-touch of the minister—
    But God's eternal vow.

His lasting testimony is: Isa. 54:10
    "The mountains shall depart
And little hills be moved away
    Before I'll from thee part."

"Your baptism is now saving you,"   Acts 38:39
    A saint said to his flock
In firm faith that God will them keep
    As safe as on a rock.

Through choice alone can they be lost,   Deut. 30:19
    Refusing God's free grace,
Or thwarting His compassionate love,
    Thus smiting God in face.

THE LORD'S SUPPER

The Lord's Supper's a Sacrament,   Rom. 11:33, 34
    Which is beyond man's ken;
It can not here be understood
    By any mind of man.

Christ came to earth as Lamb of God   Gal. 4:4, 5
    To die for sinners all,
To give His life upon the Cross,
    Atonement for man's Fall.

His Body and His precious Blood   Heb. 9:12-26
    He gave for sinful man
In order that He might him free
    From Satan's grip and clan.

By Jesus Christ came truth and grace,   Col. 1:14-22
    Which He to men revealed,
And by the sacrifice of life
    Salvation for man sealed.

The Lord of Life is here set forth   Gal. 4:4, 5
    As dying for man's sin
And in his resurrected flesh
    He comes to claim us kin.

A Sacrament He's given to us   I Cor. 11:23-26
    To draw us to Himself;
He comes right down into our life
    And gives us heaven's wealth.

Eternal life is here bestowed   Matt. 26:26-29
    When we of Him partake;
His Body and His precious Blood
    Were given for our sake.

We in partaking bread and wine   I Cor. 10:16-21
    Receive Body and Blood,
The richest gift God's ever given—
    A truly heavenly food.

Just how He gives Himself to us   Rom. 11:33, 34
    In Holy Sacrament
Is far beyond our power to know—
    It was for us not meant.

But this we know without a doubt: Heb. 6:19
    Our Lord has power to do
The things that He has pledged to us,
    For He's faithful and true.

If God can keep the shining orbs,   Acts 17:24-26
    Which roll along in space
In perfect order in their course,
    He can give us His grace.

That which God says we must believe,   Acts 4:24-28
    It makes no diff'rence "what,"
We'll take Him at His word alway
    With faith in every dot.

In Body and the Blood of Christ   I Cor. 10:16
    The Gospel is condensed;
The gift of God's full grace is there
    Each time it is dispensed.

In our communion wth Thee, Lord,   I Cor. 10:17
    Through bread and through the wine,
We have assurance doubly sure
    We're touching the Divine.

(64)

The words of Christ one must believe   Matt. 26:26
When he hears his Lord say:
"Take and eat, this is my Body—"
     He gives it e'en to-day.

Likewise the wine He offers us,   Matt. 26:27, 28
     When at the meal we sup:
"Take drink, this is the blood I shed,"
     "Drink all ye of this cup."

In this Communion with Thee, Lord,   I Cor. 10:16, 17
     We have the grace divine,
Which takes hold of our poor, weak souls
     And makes them truly Thine.

Christ gives Himself to us this way   II Cor. 12:9, 10
     For strengthening our faith,
And not alone for remembrance—
     But for imparting Grace.

A great memorial, too, is found   I Cor. 11:24, 25
     Because He's ever near
To seal the words that He here gives—
     Which drive away our fear.

The contact here He makes with us   Acts 2:42-47
     Is like a living stream;
It gives support to eyes and ears
     And makes our spirits beam.

Thus are we given power to grow   I Pet. 2:1-3
     Into a Christian life,
Which draws us from the world below—
     From all its sin and strife.

In doctrine of the Eucharist
 Chief emphasis is laid
On content of the Gospel grace,
 Which herein is conveyed.

II Pet. 1:5-8

The real presence of Jesus Christ
 Is therein clearly taught,
Which is imparted to each one
 Whose ransom Christ has wrought.

Luke 22:19, 20

The assurance of salvation free
 Is given with this seal;
The Body and the Blood of Christ
 Were given for our weal.

John 6:53, 54

They vouch for the Redeemer's claim
 That He's human-divine,
Which transcends sense and reason, too,
 Yet fulfills God's design.

Gal. 4:4, 5

When man this sweet assurance has,
 No longer can he doubt;
He knows that Christ did die for him—
 The devil he can rout.

Heb. 10:10-13

The Holy Supper is for those
 Who fix their minds on high,
Who recognize Christ's presence here
 And for redemption sigh.

Heb. 9:12-15

It's not for those who careless are
 And from mere form partake,
But for those only whose souls crave
 God's love for Jesus' sake.

I Thess. 5:9, 10

THE WORD AND PRAYER

Besides the Word and sacraments   Ps. 86:7
   We have a virtue fair,
Which is a soul-stirring fervour
   T'engage with God in prayer.

But prayer is not a means of grace,   Jer. 33:3
   Though God hears sinners' cry
And grants to them a blessing true,
   Which no one will deny.

Prayer is approach unto our God   II Chron. 7:14
   With yearning hearts' request;
And if we pray "Thy Will be done,"
   We surely shall be blest.

When in our prayer we ask of God   Matt. 6:6
   True blessings for our soul,
Them without doubt He will bestow—
   Our pleas may here be bold.

"Ye have them not, for ye ask not,"   Jas. 4:2
   Said Christ to men of old;
If to His mercy-seat we come,
   We can be just as bold.

Not every pleading of man's soul   I John 5:14
   Is true prayer in God's eyes,
But prayer that rests on God's promise
   Will raise man to the skies.

Now if we know that God hears us   I John 3:22
   When we engage in prayer,
We know we'll have the gifts divine,
   Which our requests did dare.

Wherever there's a promise given   John 15:7
    Which faith lays hold upon
And lifts it up before God's face,
    Fulfillment will be won.

Prayer is the voice of living faith   Matt. 21:22
    Pleading with tongue and heart:
Importuning God can't refuse,
    But must soul's needs impart.

When prayer to God is thus addressed,   Jas. 5:16
    Entreating food for soul,
There can not be a doubt at all,
    That prayer will reach its goal.

God works through Word and sacraments,   Ps. 86:5, 16
    Bestirring inspiration;
If we but yield our hearts to Him,
    We'll win our expectation.

By God's pure grace we gain our quest,   Jas. 4:2, 3
    Receiving what we ask,
Except when we do ask amiss
    God sees beneath our mask!

Our burdens God will lift from us   Ps. 86:7
    If we on Him rely,
Assured that He does not desire
    That we should ever die.

His Spirit thus inspires our hearts   Ps. 146:2
    And with us e'er will stay
And keep us safe within Christ's arms
    Forever and for aye.

REGENERATION

The goal towards which God's Spirit works   John 3:5
   Is man's regeneration;
The chief design He has is this:
   Effecting his salvation.

The Holy Spirit does His work   Tit. 3:5
   Upon the human soul,
Awak'ning it to life again—
   Increasing Heaven's roll.

By Adam's sin man fell from God,   John 10:10
   Became in spirit dead,
No help on earth could there be found—
   Lifeless was he as lead.

Though man when born into the world   Eph. 2:1
   Is a creature redeemed,
No faint response can he here make
   To seize that which is gleaned.

The Spirit must awaken him   John 3:5
   Through power of God's own Word;
Implanted must be a new life,
   Else his soul remains blurred.

One might as well speak to a rock   John 3:8
   As to the natural man,
If Word were not connected with
   God's Spirit, power, and plan.

If ever man is to respond   Rom. 6:11
   And to receive God's Word,
The Holy Ghost must him arouse
   Ere life in him is stirred.

To life the Spirit restores man
   Through his illumination,
And by the power the Word imparts
   Comes his regeneration.

Rom. 7:6

Darkness of soul is driven away;
   Now heaven's light does shine;
The Law and Gospel are discerned—
   And peace brought to man's mind.

Col. 3:9, 10

Where grace of God is not refused,
   Nor checked at any stage,
Man sees himself released from Law—
   Gospel's his heritage.

Rom. 6:14

He who beforehand had been dead
   Is now alive again;
A faith's implanted in his heart—
   He's freed from mortal sin.

II Cor. 5:17

In spirit he is now reborn,
   Alive is he to God;
His face henceforth is toward the sky,
   Not down upon the sod.

Eph. 4:22, 23

Along with this is here bestowed
   The power to believe,
And to pursue a righteous life—
   This power God does bequeath.

Rom. 6:22

Regeneration's a new birth,
   Which starts in point of time,
But it is not a gradual thing—
   'Tis like first sound of chime.

John 3:8

This New Birth marks the starting point,
    Bestowal of new power,
The dawning of new life from God,
    A truly heav'nly dower.

              John 8:12

The moment that the spark of faith
    First warms the human heart,
The soul's at once regenerate—
    It then is set apart.

              Rom. 6:4

From that instant it becomes just;
    It gains a holiness,
Yet not one of the mortal kind,
    But Christ's, which is faultless.

              Eph. 4:24

A warm impulse is felt within,
    Received through faith alone
Which will henceforth direct man's path
    Towards God's eternal Throne.

              Isa. 32:17

The life bestowed is Conversion,
    The turning 'way from sin
And from the power of Satan's might
    To Christ who dwells within.

              Acts 26:18

Repentance this the Gospel calls,
    Which is a change of mind,
The leaving off of sin's delights—
    Cleaving to heaven's kind.

              Ps. 119:59

Man now views things with upward gaze;
    His eyes he cast around,
And through the power of God's free grace
    His faith and love abound.

              Rom. 8:9

FAITH

Faith is belief in Jesus Christ,   I Tim. 4:10
 The Saviour of mankind,
Who came to earth to seek and save
 The spiritually blind.

By nature man is steeped in sin,   Rom. 5:10-12
 Hence is beneath God's wrath,
And if a Saviour had not come,
 He'd never find God's path.

Faith has its growth in the New Birth John 3:3
 Within the heart of man;
At first it may be very faint,
 Yet valid in God's Plan.

With increased faith Conversion grows, John 1:12, 13
 That gains in strength each day;
Faith never ceases to inspire;
 It lifts our mortal clay.

The two go hand in hand together; Rom. 6:13
 Faith is both love and trust;
Conversion is the upward climb
 Away from sin and dust.

Faith and Conversion abjure wrong; Rom. 6:6
 They cleave to God alone;
They take Him to themselves for Guide,
 Shun sin to them so prone.

Faith combats doubt of every kind; Jas. 1:3
 It is both bold and strong;
Conversion works with heaven's might
 Against all kinds of wrong.

Regeneration implants a faith
    That dulls faith in ourselves,
And leaves for us firm trust in God—
    All other trust it shelves.

Ps. 37:5

Faith binds together God and man,
    The Greater and the less;
Man makes God center of his life,
    And does to Him confess.

Ps. 125:1

The Greater takes the initial step;
    The lesser makes reply;
The latter longs to be at peace
    With Former in the sky.

Prov. 3:5

God is to faith basis of trust,
    Of holiness and right,
Foundation stone of all earth's life,
    The object of all might.

Prov. 29:25

Faith has its intellectual side,
    But chiefly deals with heart;
It's sinking of man's will in God,
    Who'll not from him depart.

I Cor. 2:5
Deut. 31:6

It never disbelieves at all
    A word that God has said;
It takes Him always as its Guide;
    It lets itself be led.

Heb. 11:6

What God's revealed must be believed;
    What He commands, obeyed;
In this relationship with Him
    No one can feel dismayed.

Matt. 9:23

By truth divine, man's soul grows strong; Ps. 64:10
 It finds its joys therein;
Through faith's continual exercise
 Man's heart is purged from sin.

All that is taught in God's pure Word Heb. 11:6
 About Himself and man
Must be accepted and confessed
 According to God's plan.

The center of God's Word is Christ; Gal. 2:20-24
 Without Him we've no plea;
If by our faith we Him receive,
 We shall the Father see.

Through Faith the Spirit offers truths Gal. 3:23, 24
 Which God's Word has revealed;
These truths man's heart at once accepts
 Though meaning's oft concealed.

"Believe on Jesus Christ, the Lord," Acts 16:31
 Is God's command to us;
And if this strong mandate we heed,
 He'll 'gender Faith from trust.

"If thou'lt confess the Lord Jesus Rom. 10:9
 And wilt believe in heart
That God hath raised Him from the dead,"
 From thee He will not part.

Receiving Him, the Christ, as Lord, Rom. 10:10
 Gives man a joyful blessing,
Which is by heaven on him bestowed
 When he kneels down confessing.

Man's faith creates the certitude   Eph. 2:8
    That 'fore God he's a sinner,
And that without power from on high
    He cannot be a winner.

Faith is the trusting hand that takes   Gal. 4:4, 5
    Firm hold on Christ, God's Son,
And cleaves to Him and Him alone
    Till travelling days are done.

When Faith binds fast the two together,   Heb. 11:6
    The believer and his God,
Man finds in Christ the power he needs—
    He's saved from Satan's rod.

Faith's certainty is not a charm   I John 3:21, 22
    Arising for display,
But firm conviction that the Christ
    Will help him if he'll pray.

It testifies to soul of man   Ps. 9:10
    That Christ is present here,
And will not fail to give him aid
    And bring his heart good cheer.

Faith often has degrees of strength,   Mark 9:24
    It may be high or low;
One ever must be on his guard
    Lest sin it overthrow.

The loss of Faith is oft portrayed   Matt. 13:15
    In chapters of God's Word;
With some this faith is not regained;
    With others it is blurred.

Repeated warnings God's Word gives   Jude 21
   That Christians watch with care
To keep the holy candles burning,
   Lest Satan them ensnare.

If there are those who have been born   II Tim. 4:10
   By Holy Spirit's work,
But now and then lose faith in Christ,
   The reason is, they shirk.

God calls to man to come back home;   II Thess. 2:11, 12
   If man heeds not the call,
And still pursues his sinful life,
   He'll get beyond recall.

Now if he falls from God's good grace   Luke 12:46
   And wills not to return,
He'll forfeit then that blissful peace
   For which his heart did yearn.

Man's ruin is from first to last   Luke 13:34
   His own determined choice;
"I would, but ye would not," says God—
   Man spurns to heed His voice.

His hostile attitude toward God   John 12:37 ff
   Is what destroys belief;
Whether or not he has been born,
   He's headed for much grief.

God's covenant remains the same;   Rom. 3:3
   When broken, it's by man,
For God is faithful to the last—
   Will keep man through life's span.

The promise that the Lord has given   I Cor. I:18
    Is one that's firm and strong;
It does not have in it a fault—
    It draws man from the wrong.

By God's own vow man is assured   Tit. 3:5, 6
    He does His will not change;
If ever broken this pledge be,
    Man does it disarrange.

Faith is a charter one can use   I Pet. 3:21
    If he has made a slip;
Not only is it good for guide,
    It rescues like a ship.

Man oft does fall out overboard   Jer. 31:31-33
    When 'tis not vessel's fault;
God's Providence is like the ship—
    "Tis safe and sound as vault."

When one falls out into the deep,   Matt. 14:30-32
    He must swim back again
And catch hold of the sturdy boat—
    And once more enter in.

Though all men were perfidious,   Rom. 3:4, 23
    Yet God's grace stays the same;
He offers still salvation free
    In Jesus' Holy Name.

The working power of such a faith   Mark 9:23
    That clings unto the Lord
Will fulfill all God's promises
    Which His Word does record.

CONVERSION AND REPENTANCE

In conversion man's soul concurs   Ps. 119:55
    With God's spirit of life
Which is embosomed in his heart—
    Which lifts him 'bove all strife.

No power has he within himself,   Eph. 2:1
    But only what's been given;
He can not by a strength his own
    Attain the height of Heaven.

Where Faith's aroused, repentance starts,   Luke 18:13
    Aversion toward all sin;
The more this Faith imbues his heart
    Conversion works within.

He hates the sin he once did love;   Eph. 6:10-17
    He now desires what's right;   Heb. 11:32-34
He's not afraid of anything;
    He's ready for a fight.

He fights henceforth the fight of faith   I Tim. 6:12
    That lifts his soul up high;
No more he grovels here below;
    He's headed for the sky.

He looks with shame and sorrow on   Rom. 6:6
    The life he once did live;
He would not now to it return
    For wealth that one might give.

Delight he finds in this new life   II Cor. 5:17
    Which Christ brings to his soul;
Through Faith, Repentance, and Conversion
    His old life's now made whole.

(78)

FAITH OF INFANTS

This question here is often asked: Matt. 18:6
     "Can infants have real Faith?"
Upon this point Scripture is clear—
     All souls are saved by grace.

The little children Jesus called   Mark 10:13-16
     Into His arms to bless,
Rebuking those that disapproved
     Who thought Christ loved them less.

Unnoticed is the infant's Faith,   Isa. 28:9
     The work of the Divine,
Who plants the germ within its heart—
     The sprouting blade's the sign.

It is not recognized at once   Joel 1:3
     By infant or by man,
But it exists in God's own sight,
     Whose eyes do all things scan.

Faith is best known as confidence,   Eph. 3:12, 17
     Staunch trust in God above;
Whether that Faith can speak or not
     Does not impair God's love.

Faith is in truth an attitude   Gal. 5:6
     Of which love is a part;
As Faith advances in its growth
     God's love is felt in heart.

Faith might be called the suppliant hand,   Tit. 3:5-7
     Receiving what God gives,
Content to be enriched by Him—
     In Christ's life it now lives!

(79)

In infant baptism Faith's begun,
    When sacrament's applied;
There is implanted then the germ
    That saves, though yet unspied.

Gal. 3:26, 27

Said Christ, "Baptize the nations all";
    Whole households were included;
In practice of the Apostles
    The child was not excluded.

Acts 16:33

With rise of Faith is knowledge gained
    As infant's mind does grow;
And to the truths, as they are learned,
    Assent follows, though slow.

II Tim. 3:15

To know and to assent thereto
    Are parts of one's belief;
Prerequisites, though, they be not,
    They're not that which is chief.

Tit. 3:5

Essence of Faith is confidence,
    Expressed or unexpressed;
It in the child is always found—
    In adults it's confessed.

Mark 9:42

Faith of infants, just like knowledge,
    And, also, just like sin,
Are all inherent in the child—
    Though unseen, they're therein.

Matt. 19:13, 14

When one's asleep, be he adult,
    Or child in mother's arm,
You could not say he has no sin
    'Cause he's not doing harm!

Acts 2:38
Ps. 51:5

Its presence real is not disproved
    Because you do not see
The knowledge, or the sin, or faith,
    Which still therein can be.

When one's baptized, there's inception
    Of sprouting faith to be,
Which will ere long be ripened out
    To full maturity.

Where Christ's Apostle certifies
    "Faith cometh by hearing,"
He there describes the usual way—
    Only what's appearing.

If plentitude of life consists
    In fully knowing God,
Then when from us death takes a child,
    It's lost beneath the sod.

But God illuminates by grace
    The little ones He loves;
He then implants Faith in their hearts
    From His great throne above.

'Tis diff'rent from a full-grown faith,
    But only in degree;
The one has ripened into bloom—
    The germ you can not see.

You would not say a babe is lost
    That passed 'way unbaptized;
Why then can't God regenerate
    A babe that's Christianized?

John 20:29

Rom. 6:3, 4, 5

Rom. 10:17

John 3:17

Eph. 2:8

I Tim. 4:10

Matt. 18:14

JUSTIFICATION

Through Faith in Christ we're justified,　　　Rom. 3:28
　　Engendered in New Birth,
Not through the root of holy life,
　　Nor man's inherent worth.

The ground of justification　　　Rom. 4:5
　　Is not found in man's soul,
But rests alone on what Christ did,
　　Who came to make man whole.

For sin Christ paid full penalty,　　　Rom. 10:4
　　Which man could never pay;
His guilt was not made null and void,
　　But justice had its day.

God did not mercy exercise　　　Rom. 5:18
　　At justice's expense,
For Christ stood 'fore the judge of men
　　And suffered sin's offense:

He paid the guilt of mankind's sin　　　Tit. 3:7
　　By dying on the Cross
That from the curse He might them free
　　And rescue them from loss.

Christ in God's sight was charged with sin;　Rom. 4:24, 25
　　Before Him man goes free;
Man has the merits Christ there won,
　　Boundless as is the sea!

It's therefore not my life in Christ,　　　Rom. 5:16
　　Nor e'en His life in me,
But only what Christ Himself wrought
　　That from sin sets me free.

(82)

All that Christ did and suffered here Rom. 4:5
 While with men here below
Is now accounted as man's own—
 God has revealed it so.

It comes to him through Christ, the Lord, Rom. 3:28
 Who while He was on earth
Kept all the Law in place of man,
 Whose efforts had no worth.

An all-sufficient righteousness Tit. 3:7
 Through Faith becomes man's own,
And in this purity so bright
 Man stands before God's throne.

In heaven's sight man is pronounced Rom. 3:23, 24
 As just before his God,
With sinful garments laid aside—
 Hence free from Satan's rod.

In his relationship to God Rom. 5:1
 Man has a newborn soul,
And at same time is justified—
 For now he is made whole.

On Calvary's Cross Christ died for man Acts 13:39
 Who was to sin so prone;
He suffered there man's penalty,
 And did for sin atone.

In Christ man's free from every sin; Rom. 10:4
 He's fully justified;
In heaven's sight he has no guilt;
 He's by his Saviour's side.

(83)

The soul of man that's in Christ born   Acts 13:39
    Is now from sin set free;
It stands before its Maker, God,
    In sweet tranquility.

God's intent for the reborn soul   Rom. 5:1
    Is man to justify;
When man stands thus in heaven's sight,
    He can not ever die.

The Holy Spirit bestows the Faith,   Gal. 2:16
    Which here effects the change;
The righteousness that man now has
    Comes from beyond his range.

Incipient righteousness in man   Ps. 15:1, 2
    Is stirred up in his heart;
When in his soul man clings to Christ,
    God doth His grace impart.

This new life justifieth not,   II Cor. 5:17
    Though holy it may be,
But only righteousness through Faith,
    The Christ's, who made us free.

Our Faith is but God's instrument,   I Tim. 6:12
    Which to ourselves we take
And wield to thwart allurements here,
    Which devils 'gainst us make.

The merits all that Christ did win   Mark 16:16
    Are ours now to enjoy;
By Faith we triumph o'er all sin
    When Christ's power we employ.

Through Faith in Christ we're justified,   Phil. 3:9
 By it and it alone;
In truth where Faith exists in heart,
 Christ's life becomes our own.

The Lord gives us the strength we need Heb. 4:16
 To o'ercome sin though strong;
If we but use the power He gives,
 We'll win o'er all that's wrong.

Man needs but fear his own weakness; Matt. 4:3-11
 He must e'er be on guard
Lest he by Satan's trickery
 Yield when he's weak and tired.

God has not e'en the least reproof   Rom. 8:1
 Against the soul of man
Who lives in Christ and Christ in Him—
 No evil does He scan.

God's thoughts are only thoughts of love Jer. 29:11
 Towards all within the fold,   I Cor. 2:9
And great rewards to them He'll give
 Who on Christ here lay hold.

Their faith in Him a temple builds   I Cor. 6:19
 In which God's Spirit dwells;
And if in His love they abide,
 They'll hear angelic bells.

Faith without works is never found,   Jas. 2:17
 God's own e'er seek the right;   I Tim. 6:12
When His Spirit directs their lives,
 'Gainst sin they'll e'er give fight.

Justification comes through Faith,
    A free, unending act,
That never ceases while Faith lasts—
    'Tis a perennial fact.

Justification e'er abides;
    In it there're no degrees;
There's nothing 'bout it incomplete—
    It shifts not like a breeze.

You're justified or you're condemned;
    Free or not from your sins;
One can not here be halfway saved—
    Either he fails or wins.

To man Christ's merits all belong,
    Or none to him at all;
If these he has, he's justified—
    Without them he would fall!

The weakest Faith can justify
    As fully as the strong;
Not so, with Sanctification—
    Reversed, when it goes wrong.

It's what Faith here accepts that saves,
    The Saviour of mankind,
Who reaches out His arms to bless,
    The sin-sick, weak, and blind.

It is the person, not the sin,
    That is by Christ forgiven;
Christ loves with a more perfect love
    Than's found in earth or heaven.

Gen. 15:6

Rom. 8:1, 30

Matt. 12:30

Rom. 8:33, 34

Gal. 2:16

I Cor. 6:11

I Cor. 1:30

SANCTIFICATION

Sanctification is begun   I Thess. 4:1-4
    The moment of New Birth,
Along with Regeneration—
    From Faith it draws its worth.

The Holy Spirit bestows belief   I Cor. 6:11
    And keeps it here alive;
It's only when the soul's reborn
    That it can ever thrive.

The Comforter whom Jesus sent   Acts 1:5, 8
    Gives strength unto the soul,
Imparts the power to do the right,
    Directs it towards its goal.

Faith's presence ever sanctifies,   Phil. 3:9
    By it life is transformed;
Where it exists it begets love—
    Thus man's life is reformed.

If in our Saviour we believe,   I John 4:19-21
    Love springs up in our heart;
"We love because He first loved us."
    His love gave us the start.

The more we contemplate our Lord,   I John. 5:1-3
    The deeper grows our love;
We feel an uplift in our souls,
    Enriched by heaven above.

E'en though God's Spirit sanctifies   I Pet. 1:7
    There's still a taint of sin;   I Tim. 6:12
The Fight of Faith we must put forth
    Or we can never win.

The love of Christ constraineth us
    To live for Him alone,
To do the right, resist the wrong,
    As He to us has shown.

His Spirit gives the strength we need,
    Bestows on us the power,
Enables us to conquer sin,
    Though tempted every hour.

As we fight on, we gain more strength;
    We grow in holiness;
The inspiration from on high
    Bestirs unbounded boldness.

Without the power God's Spirit gives,
    Who daily imparts strength,
We could not hope e'er to be saved—
    O'ercome we'd be at length.

There is no Sanctification
    Where no true Faith exists;
The two are wedded to each other—
    Herein our power consists.

In daily walk and hourly talk
    We must be on our guard
Lest from the heavenly path we stray—
    'Gainst sin we must fight hard!

Not e'en an hour dare we relax;
    Fight must we every day;
Unless Christ's righteousness we have,
    We'll miss the heav'nly way.

II Cor. 5:13-15

Eph. 4:7

Ps. 27:1-6

Ps. 33:20, 21

II Pet. 1:2-4

I Tim. 6:12

Heb. 10:31-35

Through God's indwelling love in us   Eph. 2:10
    Faith does its perfect work;
Active it is in doing good—
    It does not ever shirk.

This love of God impelleth us   Col. 1:10
    To help our fellow man,
To bring him to the Lord Jesus—
    Give succor where we can.

By love inspired holiness grows;   I Pet. 1:5-8
    Faith spurs it on and on;
When idle it is not content—
    Apart from works it's gone.

It seeks incessantly the right,   I Pet. 1:22
    Strives to become more pure,
To bring to others heav'nly joys,
    Helps human ills to cure.

When by his faith man's heart is cleansed,   Act. 7:55, 59
    He has an upward gaze;
He longs to be with saints above—
    Freed from earth's sinful ways.

As holiness on him takes hold,   Eph. 4:23, 24
    The old man disappears;
The new man daily is put on—
    Conquered are all his fears.

As long as man lives on this earth,   Rom. 3:10
    A struggle is required;
Here sinlessness can ne'er be won,
    However much desired.

GOOD WORKS

Good works as viewed from heaven above   Matt. 25:34-40
    Differ from those of man;
A good work is the fruit of Faith,
    Which follows God's own plan.

Its source and standard are revealed   Tit. 3:1, 2, 8, 14
    In God's most Holy Word;
A good work is a helpful deed
    By Spirit's influence stirred.

It's not the chosen act of man   Jas. 1:22-25
    Performed by his impulse,
But progress of the sanctified
    Where sin meets its repulse.

Within the heart it's first expressed   Jas. 3:13, 17, 18
    Then seen in outward life
In doing that which God commands—
    Thus lifting man from strife.

Where Faith exists in human lives,   Phil. 2:13
    The Spirit there does act;
In God's own Word His will's expressed—
    All we need know, in fact.

When we His holy will perform   Eccl. 12:13
    From duty we owe Him,
We've done no more than we should do—
    We've not filled cup to brim!

When you've done all that God commands,   Luke 17:10
    You have no ground to boast,
But say you are unprofitable—
    Not unblemished, at most.

(90)

Man can't do more than duty bids,   Luke 17:10
    However hard he works;
Performing less than he should do,
    That's what is meant by "shirks."

But if out of pure love to God,   Tit. 3:5
    And not for selfish gain,
A man performs his work so well,
    God's favor he'll attain.

The great God of the earth and sky,   Heb. 9:13, 14
    Who sees all things therein,
Is pleased when He observes good deeds—
    Christ's merits hide man's sin.

Reward does no man merit here,   Eph. 2:8
    That he indeed can't do;
But God's approval e'er is given
    For faithfulness that's due.

The ordinary things of life,   I Cor. 10:31
    When done for God's glory,
Are as important in His eyes
    As deeds admired in story.

The keeping of the Ten Commands   I John 3:22, 23
    Is holy in God's view
Because without the Holy Ghost,
    It's something man can't do.

The menial services of men   Rom. 14:1-23
    Are holy as the great;   II Cor. 4:17
The insignif'cant things of life
    Have an eternal weight.

Good works are service to another,   Phil. 2:25-30
    Attending to man's need;
Details of trade and household cares
    Fulfill the Scriptures' creed.

"Whate'er ye would men do to you,   Matt. 7:12
    Do ye also to them."
This is the Law and Prophets, too,
    Since days of Abraham.

To live, to speak, and to perform,   Matt. 7:8-12
    Each serving one another,
Are truly "good works" in God's sight—
    Advancing His cause further.

The common tasks should not be scorned;   Isa. 58:6, 7
    To discount them is wrong;   Col. 3:17
Superior works there can be none—
    In God alone we're strong.

Complete withdrawal from the world,   I John 1:6, 7
    As did the monks of old,
Was deemed a holier form of life—
    'Twas worse than 'mong the fold.

When man does that which God commands,   John 15:4, 5
    That's rightly called *good works;*
When with pure motives they're performed,
    No one can say he "shirks."

The things that God has not required,   Rom. 11:6
    As pilgrimage and fasts,   Col. 2:16, 17
Are not "good works" in heaven's sight—
    There's nothing there that lasts.

(92)

Such things as these God does not bless.   Heb. 9:8-14
   He does not them command;
To do them is but one's own choice—
   Yet there's no reprimand.

When you've done all that God requires,   Eph. 2:8
   There is no reward there;   Luke 17:10
You've only done what you should do—
   E'en though it's done with care.

Imperfect are good works at best;   Phil. 3:3-9
   Stained are they all with sin;
Even the best works of good men
   Can not salvation win.

When work's well done, God gives reward,   Gal. 2:16-32
   Like father rewards child;
The spirit displayed in the work
   Shows whether one's beguiled.

Reward is not by merit given   Rom. 9:16, 31, 32
   But by grace undeserved,
Which God doth shower upon His own,
   Who faithfully have served.

Pardon of sin is no reward,   Eph. 2:8
   Nor is eternal life;
God's blessings are benevolent—
   They're everywhere so rife.

God crowns within us His own gifts,   Phil. 3:7-9
   These freely He bestows,
And then rewards us for their use
   Beyond that which one knows.

RESURRECTION OF THE BODY

When Christ, the Lord, from up on high
    Returns on earth's last day,
He'll call all men out of their graves
    To stand on Judgment Day.
John 5:28

Bodies and souls will then unite,
    Become alive anew,
Appear before their Maker, God,
    From whom they once withdrew.
John 5:25

New bodies then the dead shall have
    When souls to them return;
Each corpse will then come back to life—
    There'll be no more sojourn.
I Cor. 15:35-47

The bodies that were in the graves,
    And all men who're alive,
Will hence live on forevermore—
    All will again revive.
John 5:28, 29

The upright and the knaves alike
    Will rise up one and all;
There'll be a diff'rence 'twixt the two—
    There'll then be no recall.
I Cor. 15:35

The attributes that they'll then have
    No one but God does know;
To us He has it not revealed—
    He does it not foreshow.
Rev. 20:6

The righteous will be glorified,
    Their bodies wholly changed,
Like that of Christ, their risen Lord,
    Whose power's above man's range.
I Cor. 15:50-57

Those who loved Christ shall then be clothed   Phil. 3:21
    In excellence supreme
With new immortal properties
    Beyond description's dream.

Endowed now with new faculties,   I Cor. 15:42-49
    Raised to eternal life,
They'll hence be saints in glory bright—
    Freed now from every strife.

Undying bodies they shall have   I Cor. 15:52, 53
    That need not food nor drink;   Rev. 7:16, 17
In heav'nly glory they will live
    Where spirits never sink.

As flesh and blood do not pertain   Rom. 8:17
    To heaven's life above;
The resurrected one becomes
    Heir to God's realm of love.

God will then be his all in all;   I Cor. 15:8
    Yea, all he can desire:
Beauty to see, sweet chimes to hear—
    All that he can admire.

In His great light shall he see light,   Ps. 36:10
    Shall live with Him for aye,
Adore His Son, the Lamb of God,
    Through heaven's eternal day.

Eye hath not seen nor ear yet heard   I Cor. 2:9
    The bliss of that abode
In Christ's new heaven and new earth,
    Where fears do not forebode.

With Jesus Christ, his Lord, he'll reign,
    In mansions 'bove the sky
'Mid rapturous scenes of blessedness
    Entrancing to the eye!

Rev. 5:9, 10

Jerusalem he then will reach,
    Will see God face to face,
And thank and praise Him evermore
    For His amazing grace.

Rev. 5:12, 13

Eternal life with God consists
    In visions, love, and joy
Linked by companionship with Him,
    Which nothing can destroy.

Rev. 7:13-17

The bliss the saints above will have
    Exceeds imagination;
No tongue of man can it describe—
    There's endless jubilation.

I Pet. 4:13

Like angels in the Lord's domain
    They'll occupy no space;
They'll move about as they may wish—
    No need of resting place.

Rev. 21:22-25

Not so with those who died in sin,
    Who set at naught the Lord,
Who loved Him not before they died,
    Lived not in His accord.

Prov. 1:24-31

But all who here accepted Him
    Will sit at His right hand;
The others who are on the left
    To darkness He'll remand.

John 5:29

GLORIFICATION

Glorification is the fruit   Rom. 8:16-21, 30
 Of God's Kingdom of Grace,
Which man receives in ripening form
 As he draws near God's face.

It is the crowning stage that's reached Rev. 7:9-17
 In Paradise above,
Where saints in glory and in bliss
 Extol Christ's precious love.

Regeneration's man's New Birth,   Rom. 8:17-21
 Sanctification, growth;
In Heaven glorification
 Is fruition of both.

Justification is release;   Rom. 8:30
 Man's pronounced justified,
Standing before his Maker, God,
 Without a sin to hide.

Glorification completes all;   Rom. 8:1
 Character is transformed;
Man is delivered from his sins—
 In holiness adorned.

Regained is now God's image here; I Pet. 4:13
 All sins and troubles o'er;
There's no cessation now of joy—
 It ever grows the more.

A constant progress is attained Heb. 12:22-24
 In realms of glory there,
Where new enchantments e'er abound—
 On earth none can compare!

Here man is in God's Paradise   I Pet. 1:4
    A blissful, sweet abode,
Where all is joy and happiness,
    Where fear does not forebode.

In prospect is a greater day,   Rev. 20:12
    The Judgment Day to be
When Christ with His angelic hosts
    Will set the whole world free.

At His appearing, saints above   I Thess. 4:13-17
    And all His saints below   Rev. 1:7
Will see their Lord with undimmed sight—
    All peoples will Him know.

A higher stage will then be reached   I Pet. 1:3-5
    Than that which went before,
Unspeakable the joy will be,
    And bliss forevermore!

With man's capacity to love   Rev. 1:1-19
    Increasing every day,
New revelations of the Christ
    Will unfold there for aye.

But those who Him rejected here   Isa. 5:20-25
    Must then go their own way;
The unrepentant souls of men
    Will for their sins death pay.

But those who here accepted Him   Matt. 25:34
    And gave to Him their love
Will hear with joy the blissful words:
    "Welcome! Come up above!"

Rewards that God will then bestow
   On that great glorious day
Will be conferred without favor—
   Beyond what one can say!

Rev. 2:7

In keeping with the use one made
   Of opportunity,
He'll be rewarded by his Lord
   With generosity.

Prov. 3:1, 2

The measure of one's faithfulness
   And righteousness that grew
Is not the deciding factor
   In what is now God's view.

Gal. 2:16

Relationship has here been fixed;
   The saints are in God's *know;*
But there's a diff'rence in degree—
   Some are high, some are low.

II Cor. 9:6

As one star differs from another,
   Distinction there will be;
Some souls will be quite near God's Throne
   As He will then decree.

Dan. 12:3
I Cor. 15:41

But no saint there will be displeased
   Be he far off or near;
His soul will never cease to praise—
   For heaven is full of cheer!

Isa. 12:1-6

Those who turned souls to righteousness
   Will shine as does the sun;
A special glory will be theirs
   When they their race have run.

Dan. 12:3
I Cor. 15:41

Though lips and fingers turned to dust,
    Their words and deeds remained,
And e'en though dead for many years
    They're in God's book contained.

Rev. 20:12

Some reaped their fruits while on the earth;
    Of others fruits abound
That will go on forevermore
    Wherever there is sound.

Gal. 6:7-10
Rom. 10:18

The fruits of all will there accord
    With seed that they did plant;
They'll be rewarded for their deeds,
    Be they many or scant.

Matt. 25:34-46

New bodies there the saints will have
    At Resurrection's call
When those within their graves will hear
    And rise up one and all.

I Cor. 15:41-57

Their bodies will be purified,
    Yet no doubt be the same,
Unblemished though they all will be,
    None up there will be lame.

I Cor. 15:50-53

Their eyes will see as ne'er before;
    Their ears will be more keen;
Each spirit there will stronger be
    Than e'er before was seen.

Ezek. 37:1-14
I Cor. 2:9

Endowed now with new properties,
    Freed from the reign of sin;
Glorified saints they henceforth are—
    Pure and holy within.

Rev. 7:14-17

Will saints in heaven know each other?	Luke 16:22, 23
This question's often asked;	
God's Revelation settles this—	
Up there no one is masked!	

Recall the account of Lazarus,	Luke 16:20-26
And of the rich man, too;	
The latter to the former spoke	
Suggesting what to do.	

Moses of yore and Elias, too,	Matt. 17:1-9
Communed with God on Mount:	
They knew each other, God's Word says—	
And this without a doubt!	

But one may ask, "Can one have joy	Ps. 16:11
If saved his kin not be?"	
Yes, earth's attachment is removed—	
There's nothing there but glee.	

Happiness there is undisturbed;	Ps. 17:15
The saints up there behold	
The glory of their risen Lord—	
And wonders yet untold.	

The souls in heaven adore their God	Rev. 5:11-13
So deep and, too, so strong	
That what God wills, they will also,	
Convinced God can't be wrong.	

Kinship of blood is there o'erwhelmed;	Matt. 22:29-32
It was for earthly end;	
Where there's no enmity toward God,	
Their will to Him they bend.	

(101)

The ones in glory love alone   Luke 16:13-22
    Those whom the Lord does love,
And therefore feel no yearning for
    The souls not found above.

Not so with those who're down below,   Luke 16:22-25
    Who're suff'ring for their sin,
They'd like to send one back to earth
    To warn their kith and kin.

Those living still on God's green earth   Col. 1:9-13
    Yearn those to join above,
Who, having passed on long before,
    Are basking in God's love.

The mother'll clasp her long-lost babe;   John 14:2, 3
    They'll there be intertwined;
The family circle broken here
    Will there each other find.

A blissful gath'ring there will be,   Heb. 12:22, 23
    Delightful intercourse;
They'll meet the great saints of the past,
    A mighty, heavenly force.

There all the wounds of earth are healed   Rev. 7:16, 17
    Where people were estranged;
All disagreements now are solved—
    And bliss and peace exchanged.

Unto Mount Zion they now have come,   Heb. 12:22-24
    The City of their King,
Where dwell the countless hosts of Heaven,
    Where chimes celestial ring.

Companionship of joy they form
    With all the good and great;
They learn to know intimately
    The prophets of great weight.

                                          Eph. 2:19, 20

Isaiah and Jeremiah, too,
    And all from Christ's own day,
Who knew their Lord before they died
    And e'er to Him did pray.

                                          Heb. 11:13, 32

Exalted is the thrill and joy
    When one beholds a soul
Which he himself did influence
    To seek the heavenly goal.

                                          Rev. 6:9-17

Entranced in mind and heart and will
    They converse and they sing,
And shout and praise the Lord, the Christ,
    Who them to heaven did bring.

                                          Rev. 19:5-7

One fold and shepherd there reside;
    The saints surround God's throne,
Singing their thanks forevermore
    To Christ who did atone.

                                          John 10:27-29

In that assembly of first-born,
    So far above the sky,
They're with their Saviour, Christ, the Lord,
    Who once on earth did die.

                                          Heb. 12:22-24

The songs of Moses and the lamb
    They chant in blissful tone,
And glorious are the hallelujahs
    That sin's forever gone!

                                          Rev. 15:3, 4

THE CHURCH

That Christ's Redemption be applied	I Cor. 12:28
There must be agency;	
The means through which this work is done	
Is church and ministry.	

'Tis through God's Word that grace is brought	I Pet. 2:2-5
Unto the soul of man,	
And Sacraments administered	
According to God's plan.	

When this is done, a church is formed,	Eph. 2:21, 22
A communion of saints,	
Who gather at a chosen place—	
Apart from world's complaints.	

They meet to hear the Word of Life	Acts 11:22-26
As preached in Christ's dear Name,	
To celebrate the Lord's Supper	
And spread abroad His fame.	

This Word proclaimed, they listen to;	Acts 5:42
They form themselves in group	Rom. 10:13-17
And organize a Christian church	
That their faith may not droop.	

For preaching of the Word of God	Acts 8:4-8
The Lord did His church found;	
Its mission is to plant the Word	
Throughout the whole world round.	

Within the church there's unity,	Acts 9:26-31
Bound by an unseen Hand,	
Which unites all who here believe,	
Yet they see not the band.	

The church as it is organized   I Cor. 1:2
   And as seen here on earth,
Has outward phase, but is innate—
One can not see New Birth.

External form does not suffice,   I Cor. 12:1-13
   There must be spirit's cure
To make the heart of list'ning ears
   Christlike and through Him pure.

The church's power is the Lord's Word   I Cor. 12:28-31
   Through which God's Spirit works;
The Sacraments are His likewise—
   Not used man thereby shirks!

These gifts the church brings to mankind   I Cor. 12:14-31
   In every land and age;
In form the church is quite diverse,
   But therein no strifes rage.

'Tis same Lord and 'tis same Spirit   I Cor. 12:4-13
   Who're given through the Word;
Into Christ's church they draw men's souls
   Where'er His Word is heard.

When faithfully this Word is preached,   Isa. 55:11
   'Twill be received by man;
And if to it they yield their hearts,
   It'll work its divine plan.

God's Spirit working in their minds   I Pet. 1:3-12
   Brings great joy to their life,
Moves them to spread the Gospel News
   That drives away all strife.

They meet together in loving bands,   Acts 5:42
 At first within their homes;
Later, when persecutions 'rose,
 In caves and catacombs.

A communion of saints is formed   Acts 8:25
 Who have a common bond
That unites them with one another
 Where interests correspond.

They join themselves into a group,   Acts 10:34-43
 Thus was the church begun
For carrying Word and Sacraments
 To all men 'neath the sun.

The church of Jesus Christ on earth   Acts 10:48
 Consists of men reborn,
Whose souls are linked with worshippers—
 But not with those who scorn.

Where Faith's expressed, confession's made, Rom. 10:10
 But not reverse is true,
For oft church members do proclaim
 That which they don't pursue.

Not all who join the outward church   Rom. 16:17-20
 Are foll'wers of the Lord,
But only those who're born anew,
 Who're with Him in accord.

The hypocrites are not reborn,   Rev. 20:15
 Though names are on church-roll,
But only those who are the Christ's,
 Whose names are on His scroll.

(106)

Within the church implanted thus,
    There grew an outward form,
Embracing all both true and false,
    Who confess the same norm.

God's Holy Word and sacraments
    Must be kept pure and true
So that believers everywhere
    May God's will know and do.

The unbelieving God claims not,
    E'en though they may profess
That Jesus Christ is Lord of all—
    Christ's own alone He'll bless.

If order is to be observed,
    The church must take on form,
Else much confusion there would be,
    If not a petty storm.

Subordination there must be,
    With rules and norms agreed,
As in nature and Providence,
    To make the work succeed.

A leader first must be arranged
    To take care of the flock
And lead it into pastures green,
    Or 'neath a shady rock.

His freedom here must be restrained
    For common good of all,
For there is strength in unity—
    Where not, many might fall.

Matt. 13:30

I John 1:1-5

I John 5:1, 12
Matt. 7:21-23

I Tim. 3:15
I Cor. 14:40

Heb. 13:1-7

Acts 20:28
Ps. 23:2

I Pet. 2:13

An order of arrangement stands,   I Pet. 2:13-16
    Though unwritten the law;
One dare not here set rules aside—
    Nor a false picture draw.

Where two or three believers are,   Matt. 18:20
    There is the church there found;
Established was this by the Christ,
    With whom they are here bound.

If disagreements should arise,   Eph. 5:21
    A protest may be lodged,
But no breakup must be allowed
    As long as truth's not dodged.

Throughout the ages of the past   Matt. II 13:17-33
    Since apostolic days,   Acts 15:4-31
There's been a growth within the church
    That justifies much praise.

This work is that of God's Spirit,   Mark 4:26-29
    Who guides into all truth,   John 16:13
Which lifts mankind in upward climb
    Above what is uncouth.

Developments within the church   Gal. 2:11
    Are not to be despised
Unless they should obscure the Word
    And sanction what's not wise.

The germ implanted in the church   Matt. 13:31, 32
    When first it had its birth,
Has sprouted and produced much fruit,
    Which is of sacred worth.

(108)

In doctrine, life, and government   Acts 2:41-47
   The church has made advance,
And now stands out well-organized—
   Proved so beyond perchance!

The things produced within the church   Matt. 13:16
   Are to be trusted much,   17, 31-33
And for all time to come preserved
   As work of Master's touch.

They henceforth can not be renounced   Ps. 11:3
   As long as they fulfill
The Spirit and the mind of Christ—
   And thus set forth His will.

'Fore Luther's day these were obscured,   Rom. 16:17
   The Gospel hid from view;
Corrupt were practices in vogue—
   Corrupt the priests were, too.

He cleared it of encumbrances   II Cor. 11:4, 13-15
   That held saints in their sway,
Restored to it the Gospel truths,
   Which still are ours today.

Faith is the only thing that counts;   I Tim. 4:1-3, 7
   When it is pure and sound,
It will perform its perfect work
   The whole wide world around.

United will the church become   I Cor. 12:12-28
   When all embrace God's Word
And unreservedly submit
   To truth whene'er it's heard.

A changing world the church has faced,   Isa. 9:2-7
     But true she has remained;
Through all the conflicts she has had,
     She's come through unprofaned.

Her strong fortress is her firm faith;   Ps. 46:1-5
     Hell never shall prevail;
God's in her midst, she can't be moved;
     Her power none can assail.

The vict'ry in the hard contest   Matt. 16:18
     Leans ever towards the right,
But permanent peace will never come
     Without an endless fight!

There's nothing stable here on earth   Dan. 7:14
     Except God's church alone,
Which will live on throughout all time
     Till fleeting days are gone.

When error strikes the church of God   I Cor. 14:26, 33, 40
     And heresy adheres,
A controversy is stirred up
     That marks a gain for years.

The good and evil grow together   Matt. 13:30
     In changing light and shade,
Until the end they will be found
     When separation's made.

The church down here is militant;   Eph. 2:14-21
     Triumphant it's above;
The saints who here oft wearied are
     Will there find rest in love.

THE MINISTRY

For spread of church the Christ ordained   Matt. 28:19, 20
   The Gospel must be preached
And Sacraments administered,
   That all mankind be reached.

To church is linked the Ministry,   Eph. 4:11, 12
   An institution strong
Not higher or on par with it,
   That leads God's flock along.

'Tis church's duty to provide   Acts 13:1, 3
   For teaching of the Word,
T'administer the sacraments
   Where'er the Gospel's heard.

The Ministry's an agency   Rom. 10:14, 15
   By which church work is done;
'Tis for administrative ends—
   Yet it no one should shun!

To exercise it, men are called   Col. 1:.25
   To labor, not to shirk;
While Ministry's but an order,
   It's still God's handiwork.

Possessed is church with power of keys,   Matt. 16:13-19
   To remit or retain sin;
This power belongs to entire church—
   Not to a class of men.

The Ministry's not a priesthood,   I Pet. 4:10, 11
   Yet Christ did it ordain
For expansion of His Kingdom
   And extension of His reign.

(111)

Priesthood belongs to all believers,   I Pet. 2:2-10
    To one and all alike;   Eph. 2:18
All men have right to come to God
    Whenever they may like.

No advocate is here required   Heb. 8:9-13
    Through whom to intercede;
In God's own sight they're men redeemed—
    They need no priest to lead.

To church belongs the Ministry,   Heb. 6:19, 20
    Not to members alone
But to it as an organism,
    With Christ as cornerstone.

There must be men to preach the Word,   Matt. 28:19, 20
    This is Christ's own command;   I Cor. 1:21
By preaching His atoning love
    They're saved in every land.

When for this work a man aspires   I Tim. 3:1-7
    With due preparation,
His fitness then the church decides—
    Then follows ordination.

Leader of flock he then becomes,   Acts 5:20
    Called by the church divine
And not alone from his own choice—
    When both, it works out fine!

To men the Gospel he proclaims   II Tim. 4:2
    And Law that went before;
He's called to herald all God's Word—
    Beyond that nothing more!

The Holy Word and Sacraments   Acts 5:20
    He brings them both to man;
He dare not either one omit,
    For this is God's own plan!

Without a fear he must declare   II Tim. 4:2
    The whole counsel of God,   I Cor. 4:21
Which is revealed in Holy Writ—
    E'en threaten with a rod!

The erring and the wayward, too,   I Tim. 5:20
    He sternly must rebuke,   Rev. 3:15, 16
Denounce the unrepentant ones—
    Warn those whose warmth is luke.

The sacrament he must withold   I Cor. 11:27-29
    From those that fall in sin
Till they repent, amend their ways,
    Then they may come back in.

The pastor chosen by the church   I Pet. 5:2, 3
    Which gave to him the call,
Is now God's representative—
    But not lord over all!

When in his office he performs,   I Pet. 4:10
    He works to do God's will;
If faithful he is to the trust,
    God's will he will fulfill.

No one has right to contradict   Jer. 7:27, 28
    The shepherd of the flock
As long as he proclaims God's Word,
    And stands with Christ on rock.

                                              (113)

If he, however, disregards
    The pure doctrines of truth,
He then should be dismissed at once—
    Be forced to stand aloof.
                                         Gal. 1:9

The priesthood of believers know
    When leader goes astray;
That Bible teachings be kept pure,
    He must be sent away.
                                         Tit. 1:3

This should be done with all due care;
    He must be proven wrong;
No right have they to dismiss him,
    If in God's Word he's strong!
                                   Luke 17:3

There's here responsibility;
    Each must stand on his right;
Where there's no variance from the Word,
    There should not be a fight!
                                   II Tim. 4:2

Of equal rank all preachers are
    Except in human sight;
Entrusted are they all alike
    To preach God's Word aright.
                                   I Pet. 5:2, 3

Whate'er distinction there may be
    Pertains to earthly order,
But in the eyes of Christ, the Lord,
    They all are on one border.
                                   I Tim. 4:12

The church of old used diff'rent names
    To designate this work:
Bishops, elders, and presbyters—
    Alike, as church and kirk.
                                   Eph. 4:11

The work they did was much the same;   I Pet. 5:1-3
    Their names they interchange,
Some using one, and some another—
    All worked within one range.

As long as they proclaimed the truth,   Heb. 11:32-34
    The church made strong advance,
But later when untruths arose
    They fought and took no chance!

They felt no fear, for they believed   Ps. 46:5
    The church was built on rock,
And in her straits God would help—
    Her progress none could block!

The outlook oft quite gloomy seemed   Matt. 16:18
    As if the church might fail,
But God had given His promise firm:
    "Hell's gates shall not prevail!"

Till Christ returns, He's to be preached,   I Cor. 11:26
    And Holy Supper given
To all believers 'round the globe,
    Who, fighting sin, have striven!

As time goes on the church improves,   I Tim. 6:12-16
    The good becoming better,
But oft the martyr's blood must flow—
    He feels to God a debtor.

Those who preached here with God's fervour   Dan. 12:3
    And turned many to Him
Will there shine ever as bright stars—
    Their joys will ne'er grow dim.

Part
II

Selected Subjects

of the Christian Faith in Verse

GOD'S LOVE FOR MAN

In nature and in Providence   I John 4:9
    God's love is clearly shown,
But in Redemption by the Christ
    It's crystal-clear made known.

Through Him has God declared His love,   John 3:16
    Infinite and divine,
Which brings to us who Him accept
    Life happy and benign.

The boundlessness of God's great love   Rom. 5:8-11
    Exceeds all comprehension
In that He gave His own dear Son
    For all mankind's Redemption.

This love is given us through the Christ   Tit. 2:11-14
    Who brought it from on High,
Revealing to us from above
    Our Father, God, is nigh.

Christ took man's sin upon Himself   Rom. 3:21-26
    In a vicarious way
And bore its guilt in our behalf—
    And broke for us its sway.

Such love can not be understood;   Mic. 7:18
    'Tis love beyond conception,
Love such as God alone can know—
    Outreaching all perfection.

When to our hearts this love He brings,   Luke 1:50, 77, 78
    We're lifted up on high
By Him who paid man's penalty—
    Whose love can never die.

THE PROMISED MESSIAH

Thou God didst make the earth and sky, Gen. 1:1-25
 And all things we behold:
The heavens above and earth beneath—
 Yea, more than can be told.

Praise be to Thee, the triune God, Matt. 6:25-34
 The Holy One in three,
Who cares for all Thy creatures here,
 Wherever they may be.

We thank Thee Thou didst send the Christ John 6:35-58
 To rescue man from sin,
To bring him back to Heaven above—
 That he might enter in.

Redemption Thou for man hast wrought Eph. 1:20
 Through gift of Thy dear Son,
Who took man's place and bore his sins—
 For man salvation won.

In prophesies Christ was portrayed II Tim. 1:10
 By seers as of old;
In their fulfillment He appeared
 Just as they had foretold.

Through Him Atonement has been made Tit. 2:14
 For sinful, mortal man
By sacrifice of life on Cross—
 God's grace ordained the plan.

The promised One from up on high Heb. 9:15
 In point of time did come
To open up the way of life
 And bring mankind back home.

THE BIRTH OF JESUS

The King of kings and Lord of lords   I Tim. 6:14, 15
    Has come to earth this day;
Desire of Nations, Prince of Peace,
    Will with us ever stay.

Since time began there's no birthday   Heb. 1:1, 2
    So famous and so grand
As that of our Redeemer, Christ,
    Acclaimed in every land!

For unto us this day was born   Matt. 20:28
    The Christ-Child for mankind
To save the world from curse of sin,
    To bring light to the blind.

Before He came, darkness prevailed   II Cor. 4:6
    O'er all the earth around;
There was no glimmer anywhere,
    Or light that could be found.

His coming brought to man a gift,   John 20:31
    A gift from up on high,
Announcement of deliverance
    That man no more should die.

Thus man's Redemption has been wrought   John 1:29
    Through God's beloved Son,
Who gave His life for all mankind—
    For them salvation won.

Blest be the Name of Christ, the Lord,   Heb. 13:8
    For His most wondrous love,
Who was, and is, and e'er will be
    Our Priest and King above.

THE TEMPTATION OF JESUS

In Matthew Four, verse one to eleven,   Matt. 4:1-11
    Christ's temptation is told;
The Lord was in the wilderness—
    The devil there grew bold!

When Christ had fasted forty days,   Matt. 4:2, 3
    The tempter then drew near
And undertook to win Christ o'er—
    Used Scripture without fear.

Each temptation was prefaced "if"   Matt. 4:3, 6, 9
    And each contained much charm;
The devil posed as though he had
    A Bible in his arm!

Christ claimed He was the Son of God;   Matt. 4:4, 7, 10
    Old Satan cast a doubt;
In his shortsightedness he failed—
    Christ did the tempter rout!

When in the wilderness they met,   Matt. 4:11
    A conflict did begin;
The Lord, who made the earth and sky,
    Did here o'er Satan win.

'Twas a temptation to endure,   Matt. 4:3
    For here old Satan stood
And tested Him, the Lord of life,
    Bidding stones be made food.

Temptations one, and two, and three   Matt. 4:3, 6, 9
    The devil put to Him,
But Jesus made use of God's Word,
    And thus combatted sin.

(122)

For us a pattern He has set   Eph. 6:17
    Which shows how to refuse
When Satan comes to entice us—
    God's Word we are to use.

In Eden's garden Adam fell,   Gen. 3:1-6
    Plucked fruit from off the tree
And ate of it 'gainst God's command,
    Hence man's apostasy.

But Jesus yielded not to sin,   Matt. 4:3-10
    The devil He did rout,
Proceeded then to do His work—
    And God's plan carry out.

At all times He combatted wrongs;   Matt. 4:9, 10
    Satan he drove away;
He did not show the least desire
    Him homage e'er to pay.

Jesus the Christ, true God, true Man   Rev. 15:4
    E'er was and is divine;
Not only was He without sin,
    But impeccable, in fine.

There was no possibility   Jas. 1:13
    That He would ever fall,
For His Person was the Godhead,
    Supreme Ruler of all.

Greater presumption ne'er was shown   Matt. 4:7
    Than Satan here displays,
Who tried to sway the Lord of Life,
    The Ancient One of days.

There's but one person in the Christ,
    That person's the Divine;
It could not ever be enticed—
    Or yield to foes' design.

John 1:14

In Him there's no contradiction,
    For He is God alone;
Father, Son, and Holy Spirit
    Comprise the God that's known.

John 14:16

The will of Christ is absolute,
    It can commit no wrong;
It is the standard of all right—
    Prototype of the strong.

John 5:25-29

Christ from eternity is God,
    'Tis told so in His Word;
Truly, if that we don't believe,
    Our praise to Him's absurd!

I Cor. 8:6

Asserting that the Christ could fall
    Denies the Godhead true,
Ascribes to Him mortal weakness
    Like that of me and you.

Heb. 4:15

Temptation is a test of man,
    One may or may not fall,
But that applies to humankind—
    Not to the Lord of all!

Rev. 3:7, 14, 21

If nugget's held against touchstone,
    Submitted to the heat,
It will not change if it's pure gold—
    Its purity's complete.

Mal. 3:2, 3

(124)

But we from this should not infer
    That suff'ring was not there;
The test was part of Christ's passion—
    To suffer, bleed, and bear.

                    Matt. 26:38-45

T' appreciate how Christ did feel
    With devil face to face,
You need not stretch your mind at all
    To understand the case.

                    John 12:27

Imagine only if you will
    A horrid, drunken wretch
Brought in before a refined maid—
    This picture you can sketch!

                    Prov. 23:29-32

How would she shrink on seeing him
    Come stagg'ring 'fore her feet!
And what would be her deep disgust
    As soon as they did meet!

                    Rom. 12:9

To mention them in the same breath
    Seems verily a crime!
For what pure, chaste, innocent girl
    Could e'er with such wretch dine!

                    Rev. 19:8

Now multiply this purity
    A thousand, thousandfold,
Then picture, too, the intruding wretch—
    This paints the story told!

                    Rom. 11:36

In His temptation Jesus faced
    The author of all crime
That e'er had cursed or e'er would curse
    This world throughout all time.

                    Heb. 4:15

In wilderness where they did meet
    The devil did his best,
But Christ, our Saviour, Lord of Heaven
    Did Satan's kingdom wrest.

Matt. 4:1-11

Installed was He at His baptism
    For task which He began
Of freeing man from deathly grip
    Of Satan's rule and clan.

Matt. 3:13-15

At river Jordan when baptised
    A voice pierced through the sky,
Which said, "This is my beloved Son"—
    Words from God's throne on high!

Matt. 3:16-17

As His obedient, loyal Son
    Christ was prepared for work,
Anointed for a high purpose,
    Which He could never shirk!

Matt. 4:12-17

A hard task was it to fulfill,
    But nothing could Him move;
Not all the devils in the deep
    Could His great claim disprove!

I John 3:8

"If," as said he, "Thou art God's Son,"
    Quizzed Satan in his speech,
"Isn't hunger an injustice?
    Turn magician and eat!"

Matt. 4:3

Jesus thwarted Satan's purpose,
    Asserted God's supreme;
Cost what it might, He would not budge—
    He came man to redeem.

Matt. 4:4

He had to talk with this vile wretch;   Acts 26:18
   There was no choice to make,
For He had come to take man's place
   And die upon the stake.

For man Christ paid sin's penalty,   Heb. 9:12, 15, 28
   Released him from the grave,
And clothed him in a righteousness
   That thus He might him save.

Was it not hell that He did feel   I Pet. 1:18, 19
   When He gave up His life,
Enduring tortures on the Cross
   By cruel spikes and knife?

All that was due for mankind's sins   Rev. 5:9, 10
   He paid the penalty for,
And strove to gain us for Himself
   That we might win the war.

'Gainst Satan here we have to fight,   Eph. 6:11
   Who seeks us to ensnare;
For us example has Jesus set
   How we're to do and dare.

He's given us His Holy Word,   Heb. 2:18
   The sword He Himself used
To thwart the devil's enticements—
   Lest we should get confused.

Thus making use of God's own Word   Jas. 1:12
   As Jesus Himself did,
We'll 'scape the fiery temptations—
   In Christ our lives are hid.

THE CRUCIFIXION AND ATONEMENT

Of all who've trod the earth down here,   Gal. 4:4, 5
 The Christ has no equal;
But one conclusion can be drawn—
 His whole life's the sequel.

Throughout the history of mankind   I Pet. 1:18-20
 There's none that can compare
With Jesus Christ, the sinless Man—
 His like's not found elsewhere!

There's here but one explanation   Gal. 4:4, 5
 Of this Person divine;
In truth, He is both God and Man—
 Two natures here combine.

This was His claim while here on earth,   John 17:1-3
 Its truth He did attest
When He, the High and Holy One,
 Submitted to arrest.

His life He gave upon the Cross,   Acts 2:22-24
 Dying for sinful man,
Suff'ring a death so horrible—
 More tragic none could plan!

Possessing in Himself God's power,   Heb. 2:17
 He bore the weight of sin,
The burden of iniquity,
 That heaven mankind might win!

He paid for man sin's penalty,   Col. 1:19, 20
 The guilt of entire race;
It was a burden far too great,
 No mere man could it face!

(128)

Justice divine, rightly deserved,
    Struck terror in His soul;
From cup of sin and death and woe
    He suffered here the toll.

Into the depth of that anguish
    The human mind can't go;
With crushing gloom His heart did ache—
    So deep was the deathblow!

'Twas not the pain of human flesh
    That unnerved Him on Cross,
But heaven's wrath against man's sin—
    Reclaiming him from loss.

A pall of darkness ne'er seen before
    Obstructed now the view
Which Christ, the Saviour of mankind
    Could not Himself see through!

How far the souls of men had gone
    That for them Christ must die,
The Lamb of God, man's great High Priest,
    Who came down from the sky!

The cup of death in sinner's place
    E'en to its dregs He drank
Without a flinching or complaint—
    To bitt'rest death He sank!

All this was done for you and me
    To bring us back to God,
To free us from the curse of sin
    And Satan's rule and rod.

Isa. 53:4, 5

Heb. 12: 2, 3

Matt. 27:46

Matt. 27:45, 46

Isa. 53:5, 6

John 18:11

Tit. 2:14

(129)

Freed hence is man from Satan's clutch,   Isa. 53:4, 5
    His guilt of sin is gone
If only he'll accept the Christ
    Who did for sin atone.

God's only son here took man's place   Tit. 2:14
    And died to set him free,
And now beseeches him to come
    And ever with Him be.

He offers him a righteousness   I Cor. 1:30
    To clothe his sinful soul,
Which his becomes when he believes—
    In Christ he is made whole.

This righteousness which man receives   Phil. 1:11, 27, 28
    Through his Redeemer, King,
Is all he needs God's throne to reach,
    Where sweet hosannahs ring.

When on Christ's children God looks down,   Col. 1:12, 13
    In them He sees His Son   I Sam. 16:7
And not the merits they have earned,
    But Christ's, which they have won.

Their guilt for sin He thus did pay   Eph. 2:8, 9
    By taking sinners' place
And died that they might have real life—
    Thus they are saved by grace!

In Christ alone man becomes free   Eph. 1:5-7
    And has God's blessings all,
For by His grace and Christ's merits
    He saved man from the Fall.

CHRIST'S DESCENT INTO HELL

Before the Christ arose from dead,　　　　I Pet. 3:18, 19
　　And from the grave came back,
He met the devil in his lair—
　　O'erthrew him in attack.

He proved Himself Master of death,　　　　Eph. 4:8-10
　　Of Satan and his hosts,
Proclaimed His Lordship over them—
　　Now Satan no more boasts!

Christ routed him in his own realm,　　　　I Cor. 15:55
　　Where he his captives held;
He broke the links of Satan's chains—
　　Them he no more can weld!

Christ conquered hell, death, and the grave,　　Hos. 13:14
　　Paid ransom for mankind,
By His vicarious sufferings—
　　No more can Satan bind!

Freedom to prisoners He restored　　　　Ps. 107:10-16
　　Held under Satan's sway,　　　　　　Luke 4:18
And now the peoples of the earth
　　Need no more go astray.

Redemption find they in the Christ,　　　　Matt. 20:28
　　The Son of God on high,
Who paved the way of salvation
　　That men might never die.

In Him they have eternal life,　　　　Eph. 1:7
　　Redemption from their sin;
Wide open now are heaven's gates
　　That they may enter in.

THE RESURRECTION OF CHRIST

The Lord was buried in a tomb,   Matt. 27:57-66
    A stone was rolled for door;
A guard of soldiers stood around—
    Perhaps a score or more.

On third day Christ arose from grave,   Acts 1:3
    Burst shackles of His death,
Appeared to men for forty days
    With body, soul, and breath.

By many proofs infallible,   Acts 13:31
    He showed Himself alive,
Was seen eleven separate times
    After He did revive.

With His disciples He conversed,   Acts 2:32
    With others, too, around;
They preached the great triumphant fact
    That He arose from ground.

With all their might they this proclaimed;   Acts 4:33
    They heralded it with joy;
Impelling was the miracle—
    None could the fact destroy!

In face of all who them opposed,   Acts 4:20
    Avowed they, "We must speak!"
They could not hence preach otherwise—
    No longer were they weak!

Upon this fact they staked their lives;   Acts 5:17-32
    They voiced it everywhere!
And though they suffered for their faith;
    This fact they did declare!

With gladness that none can describe   Acts 5:32-42
    This truth they did declaim,
Gave witness to it with their lives
    In words that were aflame!

Upon this truth the church was built;   Acts 5:34-42
    'Twas basis of its creed;
This one unquestioned fact they knew:
    Its sway none could impede!

"May God forbid that I should boast   Gal. 6:14
    Save in the Cross of Christ!"
Thus spake Saint Paul, the great Apostle,
    Who could not be enticed!

He knew this truth proved Christ divine,   Acts 16:5
    'Tis fundamental fact
On which the Christian church arose—
    A lie does not attract!

If Christ did not arise from dead,   I Cor. 15:4, 17
    We still are in our sin;
There's no salvation for mankind,
    Nor heaven to enter in.

Without the resurrection fact   I Cor. 15:12-18
    Redemption could not be;
We'd be without our life in Christ—
    From sin we'd not be free!

We'd have no strength to bear our load,   I Cor. 15:19-28
    No solace in our grief,
No hope at all of being saved,
    Nor from sin's sway relief!

THE ASCENSION

Foll'wing the Resurrection morn,	Acts 1: 2, 3
Christ tarried forty days,	
Speaking of things concerning God,	
And pledging heavenly rays.	

A Comforter He'd send to them   Acts 1:4
    From heaven's exalted throne,
The Holy Spirit of God's grace
    Who'd stay and be their own.

Into all truth He would them guide;   Acts 1:8
    A power to them He'd give
To witness and to spread the Word
    That all mankind might live.

Throughout the world, both near and far,   Mark 16:20
    They were to go and preach,
To carry to men everywhere
    The message Christ did teach.

While speaking thus these parting words,   Acts 1:9
    Caught up was He in air;
A cloud received Him from their sight—
    They now could only stare!

They saw two men in garments white   Acts 1:10, 11
    Who watched their gazing eyes
And said to them, "This same Jesus
    Will come some day likewise."

Back to Jerusalem they strolled,   Acts 1:12-14
    Awaiting the power on high,
The coming of the Comforter,
    Who would them sanctify.

(134)

THE COMFORTER

When Day of Pentecost was come,   Acts 2:1
    A gath'ring then took place,
Made up of foll'wers of the Christ
    Of every tongue and race.

A promise to them Christ had given   John 15:26
    Of Comforter to come,
Who'd bring back to their minds and hearts
    The truths of Christendom.

A sudden sound burst from the sky,   Acts 2:1, 2
    As rushing, mighty wind,
Which filled the house where they now sat—
    All were well disciplined.

The Holy Ghost came down on them   Acts 2:3, 4
    With cloven tongues of fire,
And sat on head of each one there,
    Which did them all inspire.

As they now spake, confused were all,   Acts 2:5-13
    Their tongues were not the same
But were of many languages—
    With joy they were aflame!

Then Peter rose and preached the Christ,   Acts 2:14-24
    Whom wicked men had slain
But now was risen from the dead—
    As God did foreordain!

He's sitting now at God's right hand   Acts 2:29-36
    And gazing down on earth,
Inviting all men to repent—
    And off'ring all new birth.

(135)

CHRIST'S INTERCESSION

At God's right hand the Christ now reigns,   Acts 7:54, 55
   High on His Father's Throne;
For us He Intercession makes
And claims us as His own.

He pleads for us, His children dear,   John 17:1-9
   That we with Him abide,
That we may never stray away—
But stay close by His side.

In our behalf He intercedes   John 17:10-17
   That we yield not to sin,
But will make conquest over wrong
And keep hearts pure within.

He prays for those who Him confess   John 17:18-24
   That they will e'er endure,   I Tim. 6:12
Keep fighting the good fight of faith
Till they their crowns secure.

His promise is to one and all   Matt. 10:32
   Who Him receive as Lord;
He'll them confess before their God
And grant them a reward.

A gift of grace is this reward,   II Tim. 1:9
   Not anything they earn,
But solely merits of the Christ,
   Who for their souls does yearn.

Rewards of merit there are none   Rom. 10:3-10
   Save what the Christ bestows,
Which as a cloak of righteousness
Is soul-cure for man's woes.

(136)

TESTIMONY TO THE CHRIST

The Christ of God, who came from heaven   Eph. 1:5-12
    Dwelt thirty-three years here,
Fulfilling all the prophecies
    And bringing man good cheer.

He did a work while here on earth   Eph. 2:8, 9
    Ner'er done by man before;
The guilt of mankind's sins He paid
    That He might man restore.

He gave his life to save all men;   Rom. 5:17-19
    For them He kept the Law
And won for them a righteousness,
    Which none as yet foresaw.

This righteousness He offers all,   Col. 1:19-22
    Who'll it by faith receive
And dedicate their lives to Him—
    They only need believe.

He taught the truths concerning God,   John 8:31, 32
    Which hidden were from view,
Unrecognized by sinful men
    Until brought home anew.

He sealed these truths with His own blood   Col. 1:14, 20
    When on the Cross He died,   John 8:46
The holy and the sinless One—
    No fault had He to hide!

He brought great blessings to all men,   Matt. 4:23, 24
    Blessings of priceless worth,
Healing the sick, the lame, the blind—
    All ills found here on earth.

(137)

He proved Himself the Saviour, Christ   John 5:33-46
   Who from the Father came,
O'er all the world it's evidenced
   When dates men want to name.

By years "B.C." and years "A.D."   Acts 3:18-24
   Most nations reckon time;
Before Christ's birth they count "backwards";
   But since in "forward" climb.

He came fulfilling prophecies,   Acts 28:23
   Made in the long ago;   John 5:39
Command gave He, "Search the Scriptures."
   There judge if claims are so.

He opened up the way of life,   I John 4:9-14
   Raised people from the dead,
Revealed to man that "God is Love,"
   Whom man before did dread.

Redemption He for mankind wrought,   Gal. 1:4
   Eternal life above,
Where saints in glory and in bliss
   Are basking in God's love.

To Him the hope of all the world   Heb. 8:9-18
   Apostles always point;
There is no other way that's known—
   All others disappoint!

The saints above and saints below,   Rev. 5:13
   The universal church,
All testify Christ is divine—
   This truth defies research!

(138)

THE SECOND COMING OF CHRIST

A day is near, Scripture reveals,   Matt. 24:29, 30
   When Jesus will return,
Will come to earth from heaven above—
   And Satan's power o'erturn.

The Second Advent of the Christ   Matt. 24:42, 44
   Will suddenly take place;
The signs ahead that will transpire
   Pertain to human race.

The Gospel shall be preached to man   Matt. 24:3-14
   All o'er the world around,
Wherever Jews and Gentiles live—
   Them all Christ yearns to crown.

"Rumors of wars" upon the earth   Matt. 24:6
   Will everywhere be heard
'Fore Christ again returns to earth—
   Known is this through His word.

"The man of sin" who's called "a beast"   Rev. 16:2
   Will rise up in his might   II Thess. 2:3, 4
And show contempt for God's elect,
   Creating fear and fright.

At call of Christ the dead shall rise,   Matt. 25:31-33
   And those alive down here,   I Thess. 4:14-17
Will all be caught up in the air,
   Where all men must appear.

According to their attitude   I Cor. 3:8, 13-15
   Toward Christ who came to save,
Freed from sin's bans they'll be received,
   Or else remain sin's slave.

(139)

THE RESURRECTION OF THE BODY
AND
THE FINAL JUDGMENT

When man's soul leaves its earthly frame His body's laid in ground Until the Resurrection morn When it will then rebound.	Rom. 5:12-15
When Christ, the Lord, from up on high Returns on earth's last day, He'll call all men out from their graves, Whose bodies did decay.	Matt. 25:31, 32
That day is near God's Word reveals, When Jesus will descend, Appear on earth from heaven above And Satan's power suspend.	Matt. 24:29, 30, 44
When He returns, the dead will rise, Bodies and souls unite; Each person will God's voice obey And rise into the height.	John 5:28, 29
All bodies that were in death's grip, And all men still alive, The righteous and the knaves alike, They all will now revive!	Rom. 4:17
New bodies then the dead will have When souls to them return; Each corpse will then come back to life— There'll be no more sojourn.	I Cor. 15:50-54
They'll come before the Lord on high In gladness or dismay And hear the sentence there pronounced On this, their Judgment Day.	John 5:25-29

(140)

The upright and the wicked, too,   John 5:28
   Will stand before Him, all,
And hear the verdict Christ hands down—
   There'll then be no recall.

According to the faith they lived   Rom. 2:5-12
   While down upon the earth,
They'll be divided into realms
   Conforming to their worth.

Before the Judge of all mankind   I Cor. 4:5
   None can the Lord deceive,
For He looks not on outward acts—
   He sees hearts that believe.

He knows all who have Him confessed,   Rev. 20:12
   Who looked to Him for life,
Who did the ways of sin forsake—
   All evils and all strife.

A separation will be made,   Matt. 25:32, 33
   His own He'll place on right,
Will welcome them into His realm—
   Released from Satan's might.

Eternal life they'll then enjoy,   Matt. 25:34
   A life with God above,
Which will not ever have an end—
   Where all is bliss and love.

The righteous ones will then be clothed   Rev. 7:13-17
   In robes of Christ supreme,
With new immortal properties
   Beyond description's dream!

The Justice that'll be meted out,
    Be it for life or death,
Will there be recognized as just—
    Pronounced by God's own breath.

Rom. 8:1, 30-34

Expelled is self-deception here;
    Mem'ry and conscience act;
Man sees his sinful thoughts and deeds—
    These he can not retract.

Tit. 1:15

His attitude toward Christ, the Lord,
    Condemns him in God's sight;
The time is spent now to repent—
    All's dark to him as night!

Prov. 5:12, 13

He's separated now from God;
    This was the choice he made;
There's no one now that he can blame—
    He must himself upbraid.

Isa. 59:2, 12
II Sam. 24:17

He chose the way of wicked men;
    Deaf ears to Christ he turned
And spurned the way of salvation,
    For which he never yearned.

Rom. 2:1

But those who hearkened to the Lord
    And him received in heart,
Are given life forevermore—
    Will not hear word, "Depart!"

John 5:24, 25

The joy that they shall then receive
    Exceeds imagination;
No tongue of man can it describe—
    It's endless jubilation!

I Pet. 2:9

(142)

Those who're accepted by the Lord   Matt. 25:34, 46
   Will sit at His right hand;
The others, who are on the left,
   To darkness He'll remand.

Upon this point God's Word is clear,   Matt. 25:31-34
   And never does it budge;   !
Christ sits at the right hand of God
   And serves as mankind's Judge.

He came to earth to save all men,   Acts 13:26, 38, 39, 47
   All sinners on the globe,
And paved the way of life on high
   By off'ring man His robe.

Christ's robe is one of righteousness,   Isa. 61:10
   Which He Himself did win
For sin-cursed man upon the earth
   To save him from his sin.

Through faith this righteousness is given,   Rev. 7:9-17
   It shields man from his guilt
And brings him into God's free grace
   Through which his soul's rebuilt.

There in his resurrected flesh   I Cor. 2:9
   He's clear from nature's change;
He'll ever have ecstatic joy
   Beyond this earthly range.

Jerusalem his home will be,   Rev. 21:4, 5, 9, 10
   Golden beyond compare,
Where God's throne and its majesty
   Surpass all everywhere!

GLORIFIED SAINTS ABOVE THE ANGELS

In God's creative Providence   Heb. 2:7
     Man stood in second place
To angels, ministers of God,
     Who serve the human race.

Outdistanced now the angels are   I Pet. 3:22
     Through Christ born here as Man;
Assume did He a human form
     That He might lift sin's ban.

In kinship with Divinity   Heb. 2:5
     Man now stands in first place
Above the angels in God's realm—
     Saved by His Saviour's grace.

Man thus exalted by the Christ   Heb. 2:6-18
     Surpasses angels' height,
And now stands out more glorified
     In heaven's celestial light.

The angels who were next to God   Ps. 104:4
     Before Christ came to earth
Were spirits only by kinship—
     Not changed by a new birth.

But man with body, mind, and soul,   Matt. 24:31
     Redeemed by Christ divine,
Was lifted to a higher life—
     This was God's own design.

Clothed was the Christ in human flesh   I John 3:1, 2, 10
     To rescue man from sin;
Man thus redeemed is higher raised—
     To God he's doubly kin!

(144)

THE ONE ESSENTIAL FOR SALVATION

In countless ages 'fore man came   I Pet. 1:18-21
    To live here on this earth,
The great God in His wisdom planned
    To give to man new birth.

In His prevision He foresaw   Ps. 106:8
    That man would go astray,
Would fall from his holy estate—
    From sky to mortal clay.

When God created man at first   Gen. 3:1-19
    He gave to him free will,
To do as he desired to do—
    Be that choice good or ill.

But 'neath temptation man did fall;   II Chron. 29:6
    He lost his purity,
And in his sad and sinful state
    Had no security.

Away from God man turned his life,   Isa. 59:12-15
    Pursued a downward path,
By sinning fell away from grace,
    Was now beneath God's wrath.

In pity God looked down on him,   Luke 15:17-21
    The creature of His Hand,
Him to release from curse of sin—
    Bring him to a happy land.

God's only Son came down to earth,   Acts 10:36, 43
    Who would all men redeem
And draw them up to heaven above
    Where pure bliss reigns supreme.

(145)

The Christ appearing took man's place,   I John 2:1, 2
    A substitute became,
To pay for sin its penalty
    And thus did man reclaim.

A Saviour He became for man,   Eph. 2:13-18
    Invited all to come,
Partake of riches of His grace,
    And find a peaceful home.

Redemption has man in the Christ,   Rom. 5:1-11
    Forgiveness of his sins;
Through God's great mercy and His love
    Man here a pardon wins.

A restoration's given him,   Rom. 5:15-21
    A new triumphant life,
Which raises him to heavenly heights
    Where there can be no strife.

Through Christ God gave His Holy Word: Acts 26:18-22
    All that man needs to know
Concerning life here and hereaft
    To save from endless woe.

This Word exhorts, "Believe in Christ,   Rom. 4:3-24
    Receive Him in your heart,
Accept the righteousness He gives,
    And ne'er from Him depart."

If you believe you shall be saved,   Mark 16:16
    This is His promise sure;
If you but take Him at His Word,
    Your soul will be secure.

For you the Saviour paid the debt   Rom. 10:4-12
    Which you could never pay;
If you accept Him as your own,
    You'll happy be for aye.

But one condition is required: John 3:16, 17
    Receive Him in your heart,
Believe in Him with all your might,
    Then from you He'll ne'er part.

"He that cometh to Me," said He,   John 6:37
    "I'll never Him cast out,   Isa. 45:22
Look unto Me and be ye saved"—
    No room's left here for doubt.

Accepting Him, you will be safe;   I Thess. 5:9, 10
    No one can do you harm;
No fears nor foes can then disturb—
    Or cause the least alarm.

The heavenly mansions will be yours;   I Cor. 2:7-9
    Your joy will be complete;
For bliss and ecstasy abound
    Around the mercy-seat.

"As I live," saith the Lord, your God,   Ezek. 18:32
    "In death I have no pleasure";
If you'll receive the life He gives,
    Your joy will have no measure.

The one essential for your life,   Eph. 2:4-10
    The safety of your soul,
Is *faith* in Jesus Christ, your Lord—
    Through Him you'll be made whole.

THE SCOPE OF SALVATION

The boundlessness of God's great love   I Tim. 2:4-6
     Is everywhere proclaimed;
It's seen in nature all around—
     And by God's saints acclaimed.

The wondrous depths of that great love   Eph. 2:4
     Surpasses human thought;
No other love in all the world
     Has such amazement wrought.

The race of man from Adam down   Rom. 8:31-39
     In every age and place
Is loved by God who made them all—
     All men are saved by grace.

Provision has been made for all   Ezek. 37:23
     For rescue of mankind
By Jesus Christ, God's only Son—
     All who're sin-sick and blind.

That God should give His only Son   I John 4:9
     To die for sinful man
Is foremost fact that's been revealed
     Within Redemption's plan.

The Saviour died to save mankind,   I Tim. 2:3
     And not for just a few;
He is the Saviour of all men,
     Including me and you.

"Look unto Me and be ye saved,   II Tim. 1:9
     All ye ends of the earth,"   Isa. 45:22
Said God through His prophet divine—
     Here's offered man new birth.

(148)

What more assurance could be given   Rom. 5:1-5
    To sinners on this globe
Than that which Christ here offers all
    Who will accept His robe.

"Come unto Me and be ye saved"   I John 4:9-10
    Is His pleading appeal,   Isa. 45:22
Held out to one and all alike
    And sealed by vows most real.

"Ho! Everyone that thirsteth, come,   Rev. 22:17
    Come drink that ye may live";   Isa. 55:1
He bids man quench his thirsty soul;
    Water of life He'll give.

"Although your sins as scarlet be,   Isa. 1:18
    White shall they be as snow":
This affirmation God here gives
    To all mankind below.

Commissioned are God's people all   Matt. 28:19, 20
    To carry Word of life
Unto the nations on the earth,
    Who live in sin and strife.

This mandate given by the Christ,   Luke 24:46, 47
    Who spent His life for all,
Has but in part been carried out—
    Not all have heard His call.

'Tis not the fault of grace of God   Deut. 6:6-9
    Whose Spirit is world-wide,
For He all mankind seeks to save—
    No man dare His Word hide.

Those who are living without Law
　　In heathen lands and climes,
Who have not heard the Gospel News,
　　Will they miss heaven's chimes?

Isa. 45:21, 22

Those without Law are judged without,
　　Within Law judged within;
The Lord and Saviour Jesus Christ
　　Died for the whole world's sin.

Rom. 3:10-29

Infinite was the penalty paid
　　By Saviour of the race;
All humankind was thus redeemed
　　From sin and its disgrace.

Eph. 1:3-12

Impelling is our duty here
　　To spread abroad the news
That's been revealed in Jesus Christ—
　　Failure does not excuse.

I Cor. 9:16

If we this duty don't fulfill
　　And ears to hear don't hear,
Will that be held 'gainst those without
　　Who breathe same atmosphere?

Rom. 10:14, 15

Would we not be incurring blame
　　And sinning 'gainst our soul
If we our duty failed to do,
　　And mankind's not made whole?

Ezek. 33:7-9

Where sin abounds, grace more abounds,
　　Said Paul, the foremost teacher,
Who save the Christ, man's Redeemer,
　　Was world's greatest preacher.

Rom. 5:20
I Cor. 2:4, 5

God has ordained that all shall hear   I Tim. 2:4
    And learn of Him the way
By which salvation is attained
    While on the earth they stay.

If some don't hear while others do,   Rom. 2:11-16
    That is no fault of Him;
It's naught but man's remissness here—
Not God's whose love's not dim.

The Christ, who died for all mankind,   I Cor. 3:11-23
    Died both for you and me
And all the others in the world
    Wherever they may be.

The devil and the demons all   I Pet. 5:8, 9
    Have only finite power;
They're not creators of our life,
    Nor can they life devour.

'Tis true they fight an endless war,   Rev. 12:7-9
    And have a mighty strength
To enslave men and drag them down—
    But this bout has its length.

They go so far, then they must stop,   Rev. 12:10-11
    They're 'neath high heaven's sway,
And though world-wide in their assaults,
    They have at last their day.

There's but one Master in the world,   Rev. 19:1
    And that is God alone;
Not all the powers in universe
    Can ever Him dethrone!

(151)

"Praise God from Whom all Blessings Flow!"   Ps. 107:8

The universe and heav'nly hosts   Exod. 15:11-18
   With speechless voice proclaim
In breathless tones to men on earth
   The praises of God's Name.

Without God's everlasting strength,   Ps. 90:1, 2
   Imparted every day,   Ps. 104:29-32
We could not breathe or love or hope—
   Nor could we ever pray.

We'd be o'ercome in deep despair,   Ps. 143:7
   If God we could not hear,
Who speaks to us in nature's realm—
   And through His Word so clear.

In Christ we are His very own;   Rom. 6:16-18
   If we our hearts will yield   Isa. 40:31
And serve Him joyously down here,   Ps. 33:20
   He'll be our strength and shield.

And in the mansions up above,   Rom. 6:22, 23
   When we shall come to die,
He'll us receive and welcome home—
   Then joys will multiply!

These joys will increase and abound   Luke 6:23
   Throughout the aeons of time;
With angels and with saints we'll dwell
   In blessedness sublime.

"The life above, the life on high"   Rev. 21:1-7
   Is love and bliss supreme;
All fears and sorrows are dispelled—
   Entrancing as a dream!

(152)